THE HEART
OF ALL
KNOWING

First published by O Books, 2007
O Books is an imprint of John Hunt Publishing Ltd.,
The Bothy, Deershot Lodge, Park Lane, Ropley, Hants, SO24 0BE, UK
office1@o-books.net
www.o-books.net

Distribution in:

UK and Europe
Orca Book Services
orders@orcabookservices.co.uk
Tel: 01202 665432 Fax: 01202 666219 Int. code (44)

USA and Canada
NBN
custserv@nbnbooks.com
Tel: 1 800 462 6420 Fax: 1 800 338 4550

Australia and New Zealand
Brumby Books
sales@brumbybooks.com.au
Tel: 61 3 9761 5535 Fax: 61 3 9761 7095

Far East (offices in Singapore, Thailand, Hong Kong, Taiwan)
Pansing Distribution Pte Ltd
kemal@pansing.com
Tel: 65 6319 9939 Fax: 65 6462 5761

South Africa
Alternative Books
altbook@peterhyde.co.za
Tel: 021 447 5300 Fax: 021 447 1430

Text copyright Barbara Meiklejohn-Free 2007

Design: Stuart Davies

ISBN: 978 1 84694 070 5

A CIP catalogue record for this book is available from the British Library.

Printed in the US by Maple Vail

THE HEART
OF ALL
KNOWING

Barbara Meiklejohn-Free

The Highland Seer

BOOKS

Winchester, UK
Washington, USA

This book has been the greatest healing and teaching of my life, it is from my heart to your heart, from the Heart of the universe.

DEDICATIONS

To Swain McDonald, the Highland Seer, for without his help and influence in my life this book would never have been written.

To my Mother Doreen and my Father Bill, now in the spirit world, you are only a thought away.

To Grandfather Wallace Black Elk, elder, shaman and seer. It is an honour to know you.

To Betty Shine because she has had such an influence on my life, from the Spirit world, and to Mary Duffy, a wonderful medium from Scotland, you are sadly missed.

CONTENTS

FOREWORD

Connection to nature, the intuitive state and a sense of knowing are all manifestations of something much deeper and something that has been held sacred by adepts and seers throughout time. Often this deeper sense has been secret - for those with the eyes to see. The reasons may vary throughout time, but one of the most perplexing reasons is the fact that not everybody understands what they are seeing, hearing or sensing.

To some, the senses are open from a very early age. To others they remain forever closed. Our ancestors understood these open and closed minds and understood that language or symbolism could hide or reveal the truth. For myself, I have spent many years deciphering and decoding this ancient and sacred language, but Barbara is one of those individuals who can just know. Her in-built senses were open from a very early age and have not just remained open, but grown with time and knowledge. True wisdom is not just about learning from books and neither is it just about experience. True wisdom is the union of the exoteric with the esoteric, the outer with the inner. The seers sense unites both these outer and inner worlds in a way that mankind and indeed womankind has done for millennia.

This book is the journey of that sacred path. It is the revelation of a true seer and within these pages you will find true wisdom. Ultimately what you shall discover is the journey of the mind, the soul and spirit, back into the heart of the mother of all - nature itself.

Philip Gardiner

Author of *Gnosis, The Ark, The Shroud* and *Mary and Secrets of the Serpent*

PREFACE

Like many of you, I often get confused by reading a book. That is why my book is simple. It is my life's work. I speak to your heart because the words come from my awakened heart, the heart of a seer. I am writing to reach out to every single one of you to affirm that you already have the gifts and abilities of a seer within you. I will help you find your own inner teacher, reclaim your personal power, and remember the sacred knowing that has been with you since the beginning of time. Together we will face and overcome the fear of knowing yourself.

During my travels, I have met many friends who share my dyslexia. I have experienced how terrible it is at school to be called stupid and much worse, and to be beaten by teachers for not being able to write. I understand now that some of us are given this great gift so we can excel at learning our oral traditions, the heart talk that our ancestors passed on to their kin.

In this book, we revisit our roots in our many homelands to reconnect to who we are. The information is from my experience, working with the spirits of living forces in many lands. I feel especially honoured to share with you the awakening experiences of my formative years living in the rugged, magical Highlands of Scotland.

I have remembered myself by listening, feeling, walking on the land, and working first-hand with indigenous peoples. I have accessed the inner knowing of my past, present, and future lives. I have celebrated my healing with a sacred marriage to myself. I have learnt to transform anger, grief, pain, and the unnecessary burdens of doubt placed upon me by others into a great masterpiece of life.

I came back to Egypt to write this book and to reconnect with the ancestors who appeared to me in my very first past-life vision. Greeks, Romans, and Hebrews among many other people throughout history have traveled to Egypt searching for knowledge. The oral traditions have not been lost here. They are learnt from every rock and tree, the wind, the sun, the elements and from each animal and creature which coexists within and without the ancient temples that appear and disappear among the desert sands like ships on a rolling sea. These teachers of our nature are the tools and medicines of seers today because the Earth has not forgotten who we are.

Great seers and shamans are alive and seemingly dead, without as well as within you, awaiting rediscovery. This book will help you understand that everything happening to you at this moment in time is for a purpose.

I am asked what I have learnt most from all my travels working with shamans and medicine people, and the answer I give is "how not to be." We know when we feel imposed upon, or perform our work as a duty instead of as a joyous expression of what energizes and enlivens us. It is time to wake up from who we are not, and become who we were born to be. Who were you before you forgot?

Welcome to the seer's worlds of miracles and magic. We know the answer to the only worthy question: who am I? Deep inside us is the will to know the truth of who we are. That answer comes from our wise spirits. This forbidden knowledge is kept from us by many means, for if we were to discover this secret it would empower us beyond belief. In this book, I will empower you beyond belief by helping you remember your beautiful soul.

You will find the Holy Grail and Great Spirit you have been searching for all along. You will awaken from your self and see our Earth from *The Heart of All Knowing*.

Blessed Be
Barbara

INTRODUCTION

In this lifetime I was born in the ancient Highlands of Scotland. My first memory is of awakening in my bed one dark night when I was three years old. I saw a man standing at the bottom of the bed with feathers in his hair. He was dressed in what I now know to be Native American clothing. He spoke to me and told me he was my Spirit father. He was here to help me understand who I was and where I had come from.

This was the beginning of many visits from the Spirit world. I was never afraid because they were my family. They cared for me in a way my parents could not, for my mother and father had been conditioned from their childhoods not to love themselves. As parents they struggled to express their love for me. So, my journey was one of learning the hard way. At home I was not understood, at school I was beaten and even stoned because I predicted things. When I was sent to church I saw spirits of dead people and told the congregation about their relatives. Again I was beaten. However, no one could take away my spirit.

Then, at twelve years old, I met Swain MacDonald, the Highland Seer. I had encouragement from him to know who I was because as a seer Swain knew me as I remembered myself to be even before I was born. He took me to the sacred places on the land that my ancestors walked upon. I connected to their spirits and to all the elements of Nature. I was often visited by ravens and crows when I worked with the weather, so Swain gave me the Spirit name of Raven.

As I am writing these words, a raven has just come onto the terrace where I sit. Our connection to Nature is never lost. I wrote Raven, I thought raven, and a raven visited me on his way to the Nile.

When we are ready our teacher, guide, and friend appears. Some people think that a guru or master will all of a sudden turn up in front of them. It is true that this experience happens to a few of us, but it occurs most often when we have been students of life and have gained experience from life itself. Then our inner wisdom is revealed to us. For this great awakening our teacher manifests to encourage us to go even deeper within and more gratefully without, as Swain did for me.

Adventures of many lifetimes are encoded deep within us. Some of us remember our experiences and carry them forward into this lifetime. People often ask me how it is that I remember so much. As a dyslexic I do not retain thoroughly what I read. The simplest answer is that I already carry wisdom within me from previous lifetimes. Seers remember our connection with Spirit and Nature. I have walked the timelines and have revisited my past lives through visions. I have remembered who I am, where I am going, and how to get there.

Some of us remember who we are when we come into this lifetime, and remain willing to carry that remembrance forward until we are sure of its truth. Even those of us who have forgotten our inheritance are still feeling and sensing the remembrance, triggering the mind to think, "Oh, I can't be so stupid and egotistical, that can't be me. That's not possible." It is. We have all walked the ancient ways in previous lifetimes. We have had experiences of being the medicine man and the wise woman. We have lived lives as Native Americans, Mayans, Egyptians, Celts, and other ancient cultures.

A seer works through feeling, our first sense. Fear is the human body's last sense, our mind's first nonsense. Throughout my life, Spirit has taught me that the way of knowing is always through the heart. Simply reading about the techniques and tools of seership will not make anyone a seer because that type of enquiry comes from the practical mind. Seership is the practice of feeling and willing the presence of Spirit and Nature through our hearts. Real teachers and the true masters do not need to call themselves so, nor do they have need for names. I have found just such amazing people in many parts of the world. They live simply. Their universal wisdom always feels like a very personal gift. Seers remember that all our gifts and abilities come from our Father in Heaven and our Mother Earth.

Mediums and psychics feel the Spirit world and its conditions. Each of us can get in touch with our feelings and emotions and recognize which are our feelings and which are the feelings of the Spirit and natural worlds. It is the same experience as when we detect emotions from people around us. Some days we feel sad and yet we know that it is not our sadness. It could be the sadness of someone close to us, or perhaps we are experiencing the feelings and emotions of the Earth.

Since childhood, I have been aware of earthquakes and volcanic activity. I knew, sensed, and felt when the last Californian earthquake hit. I know when there will be extraordinary seismic activity because I feel the Earth. I am connected to the Earth because I am in tune with and in balance with Spirit. Seers share such understanding of Nature and Spirit with others during their readings.

Seers live and feel from our all-knowing hearts. Our ancestors knew to do what Spirit wills and Nature reflects, to harm none unnecessarily and to cooperate with others. We may have missed the lessons of love and interconnectedness in our earlier family lives and schooling. Yet, when we love others as if they were our own brothers and sisters, we remember how to love our own spirits and souls. There are no two people alike in all their physical, mental, emotional, and spiritual expressions. Every body is individual, every thing is different and every person that comes to a seer for a reading is unique.

When I walk around psychic fairs today, I visit many mediums and psychics who are doing good work. However, I see the gap of a table between their clients and themselves. Psychic and emotional contact with persons during a reading often becomes physical as well. Seers care when the person having a reading starts to cry because someone from the Spirit world comes through to them with a message. Seership is not just about the message. Seers are messengers, ambassadors for Spirit. Spirits want to touch, hold and hug their loved ones and tell them that they love them through the clear channel of the seer. This intimacy is difficult to achieve with a table or the distance of a medium's platform separating the messenger from who the message is for.

Seership is not work that can be easily switched on and off. Seers live and walk with spirits and souls in Heaven and Nature. We are here to help people during their times of sorrow. We understand how they feel because we share their soul's feelings but not their self's emotions of pain and fear. We offer our knowledge of the unity of the worlds to help others get through times of disconnectedness. We use our gifts of natural sensitivity and spiritual awareness for reaching, touching, and caring for human beings on this Earth.

Seers know how to help unease and disease. We travel beyond the ordinary world of selves into the worlds of spirits and souls to know whether a physical ailment such as a bad back also contains relevant mental, emotional, or spiritual messages. As healers, seers heal our own selves, whether we schedule ourselves as our first or last patient. There are many healers in the world today because we are all teaching and practicing what we desire to learn and perfect in ourselves.

A seer does not tell fortunes because predicting the future is declaring what must happen. Many of us are taught fate and karma, yet we actually create and recreate our own destinies. We manifest Heaven on Earth by waking up to the souls and spirits we are right here and now. Look around your home for clues of who you were and will be. What do you enjoy doing? What are you interested in reading more about? Do you rely on your intuitions and instincts for guidance?

When you put into practice the gifts and abilities that I am reminding you of in this book, your psychic abilities will develop and become clearer and stronger with practice. You will use these gifts and abilities to see beyond this world of selves. We will weave between the worlds of selves, spirits and souls. You will trust your heart's feelings and knowing and become aware of how you honestly experience the many things that seemingly happen to you all the time.

In this book, I share my life stories about seeing our Earth through eyes of the all-knowing Heart. I see our Earth by sensing my heart. All of us are able to sense our hearts by finding, remembering, and dreaming our souls. Seers are ready to find, remember, and dream our souls by trusting and hearing our spirits. We are willing to trust and hear our spirits by loving and healing our selves. In harmony with all natural traditions of heavenly purpose, we prepare to love and heal ourselves by honouring our ancestors.

CHAPTER 1

HONOURING OUR ANCESTORS

Seership is living with the miracles and magic of everyday life. It is a natural and spiritual way of living. Seers listen until we remember our constant connection with the vast universe, regardless of our seemingly insignificant individual life paths. When driving along a road we are still connected to Spirit and Nature. Seers merge with our insights and visions to become one with the destiny they reveal.

Even before our ancestors lived in caves, wise men and women honoured the sun each day, observed the synchronicity of the moon cycle with terrestrial activities, and patiently noted the correlation of the procession of our stars to human events. We gained our outer wisdom directly from Heaven and Nature, and listened to the wise ones who helped our doubting minds and busy bodies receive our heart's divine inheritance.

We have variously called our wise ones seers, prophets, shamans, sheiks, sages, guides, mystics, saints, masters, gurus, medicine men, magicians, and witches. As witnesses to the divine manifestations of our Heart, seers use our intuitions and feelings to translate the seeming mysteries of the universe into the vernacular of our communities. We simultaneously develop our wisdom and compassion by recalling our soul's past incarnations. Seers retain from lifetime to lifetime our heart's answer to "who am I?" When our reconnection to all worlds is completed, the seer is ready to share our mastery of the mystery of Spirit and Nature.

For most of our history as human beings, we have expressed ourselves orally and symbolically. Today we call this way of understanding "right-brained" to distinguish it from "left-brained" skills like writing and analysis. The ancients also knew of these two ways of understanding, referring to them more simply as the pathways of the inner and outer mind, or the worlds of the heart and self, respectively. The oral traditions or "heart talk" of our ancestors still exist among the aboriginal peoples of Australia and New Zealand, the native North and South Americans, the African tribes and their Caribbean cousins, Asia's diverse animist communities, and the resurgent European pagan culture.

Much later in our development as societies, we began recording our wisdom in the form of pictures and hieroglyphs. Seers existed for thousands of years in the ancient mystery schools of Egypt, Greece, and Babylon. Ancient Egypt is the land of the oldest forms of magic and is the source of oracular wisdom. Oracles are prophesies and also refer to the temple and the priestesses and priests who impart the divine messages. Egyptians honoured the priests and priestesses of the ancient gods and goddesses. They underwent intense mystical training for many years, forfeited personal goals and belongings, and lived in near solitude. The High Priestesses or Priests were the masters of seership gifts and abilities.

At Heliopolis, the major religious centre for the cult of Ra in ancient Egypt, one of the titles for the High Priest was the Great Seer. Every Pharaoh in every dynasty had a Great Seer to consult on natural and supernatural timings to coordinate worldly events. This arrangement continued until 664BC when Egyptian rule reverted to foreigners.

Ancient Egypt had no analytical sciences. Instead, the people relied on the inner wisdom and knowledge of their Pharaohs and seers. One seer whose name survives is Horwedja, the Great Seer of Heliopolis. He built a chapel for healing at the temple of Mut in Karnak to honour the divine Votaresses, goddesses who were the god Amun's wives. However, the greatest seer of ancient Egypt was Imhotep, meaning the one who comes in peace. He was a doctor, scribe, poet, astrologer, and architect of the pyramid complex at Sakkara.

Our ancestors eventually organized their symbolic understandings of the outer and inner worlds into ever more abstract forms of writing. The Greek historian Herodotus became a wisdom keeper of the mystery schools of his day. He followed his vision, travelling to Egypt and recording in writing their ancient oral traditions and temple practices. The

Greeks traveled by the thousands to Egypt and the Far East seeking wisdom of the ancients, and as a result of their earnestness many Greek seers are recorded in history. Greek priestesses called Sibyls were the seers of the Oracle at Delphi, home of the Goddess of Creation represented as the Earth's womb.

Pythagoras is remembered in the West for his brilliant codification of Nature's geometric patterns. He awakened as a seer through initiations into the Egyptian, Chaldaean, Orphic, and Eleusinian mysteries. His genius combined the rapidly evolving Greek intellectual sciences of the questioning mind with the eternal spiritual answers of his all-knowing heart. Plato continued Pythagoras' synthetic work under the guidance of the profound sage and seer Socrates.

Socrates was executed in his prime for his commitment to philosophy, literally for his devotion to Sophia, the goddess of wisdom. Plato's dialectical methods re-engaged the mind to the heart by proving that our initiate learning of the supreme mysteries is actually our reminiscence of universal inner wisdom. Plato recorded Socrates' delight in demonstrating the power of compassionate insistence to awaken psychic gifts in ordinary persons.

The Chassidim and Essenes were Judaic mystery schools that combined strict physical disciplines from their school of prophets with the spiritual wisdom of the Babylonians. Philo was a Judaic seer who studied with the Therapeuts, a cult of seers and philosophers who lived simply with Nature. They healed body and mind through their knowledge of emotional stress and spiritual distress.

In the most ancient biblical texts, seership is a special gift from Heaven. Many seers are recorded in the western Bible before and after the prophet Samuel who lived over 3000 years ago. Mediaeval Cabalism invoked the vision of Ezekiel many hundreds of years after its recording in the Bible. John the Baptist was a renowned seer who foretold the coming of the influential seer Jesus. The prophet Mohammad believed that there were over 120,000 biblical prophets or seers who preceded him, beginning with Adam and including Noah, Abraham, and Moses.

Renowned seers of the West include Nostradamas and Edgar Cayce. Nostradamas was born in 1503, yet knew of the rise and fall of Napoleon, the antichrist "Hister" and World War II, the recent collapse of the Berlin Wall, and much more. Edgar Cayce, the Sleeping Prophet, was born in the USA in 1877. He foresaw both World Wars, the Wall Street crash in 1929, and the creation of the State of Israel. In October 1935, he spoke of the forthcoming holocaust in Europe.

Martyrdom became the heart-wrenching destiny of many seers in historical times. Religiously sponsored genocides during the appalling era called the Middle Ages prematurely ridded this world of inspiring saints and seers, one of whom was the courageous Maid of Orleans, Joan of Arc. Our last century witnessed the horrid destruction of millions of innocents in Europe, Africa, and Southeast Asia. Too numerous to contemplate among the departed souls are the seers of these cultures.

I must also mention the killing of thousands of seers in America during its relatively brief history. Women seers were burned as witches, Native shamans were exterminated as savages, and visionary politicians were executed. One seer whose impassioned vision continues to grace the American multicultural dream is Martin Luther King. He had the inner knowledge of his impending assassination, yet continued his divine mission with unparalleled dignity.

Amid these daunting losses, the seership thread continues to weave itself among native peoples of today's world. The Highland Celts are one such clan that I am blessed to be born into and my heart forever remains joined to this beautiful womb of the Mother. The Highlands of Scotland have been for centuries the last bastion of attempted conquests. The land gifts us with stout spirits. Hundreds of standing stones and other sacred ruins grace the British Isles; they date from at least the time of the Druids and hold powerful ceremonial energies of the ages. Our ancestors' wisdom resides in these rocks, awaiting an eager heart to listen to their truth.

Seership flourished among the Celts. The most famous Celtic seer was

Kenneth Coinneach Odhar Mackenzie, the Brahan Seer, who was born in Scotland at the end of the 17th century. He foretold the Battle of Culloden in 1746 and the genocide attempt by the English against the Scots during what are now called the Highland Clearances. He also foresaw the invasion by Hitler of Poland and its subsequent downfall. This Highlander's second sight caused his own excruciating death in a burning tar pit as retribution for an indiscretion that he was obliged to divulge.

Long before I could fully appreciate my fortunate birthplace, I remember as a child of about four or five having visions as I stared into the fire on many long Inverness winter nights. I was reminded of this experience when recently viewing the film version of C.S. Lewis' *The Lion, the Witch, and the Wardrobe*. The little girl of the same age sits listening to flute music and all of a sudden has visions from within the fire. There are many wondrous things that we experience as children, yet forget or dismiss later in life.

At eight years of age, I knew exactly what I wanted to do. I told my mother that I could not learn what they were teaching me in the primary school because I already knew what I needed to know. I was outside in my classroom of Nature as much as possible. I saw, heard, and felt everything in Nature. Animals, trees, the wind, thunder and lightening all spoke to me. When I went to the school, I could not understand their strange thoughts about things I already knew, or about which I had no passion.

Later I realized I had Nature as my school in many other lifetimes. The sun, moon, stars, and the elements of wind, water, fire, and earth were my familiar teachers. I once picked up a leaf and my Spirit guide told me that this leaf contained more knowledge than a whole book. The spring, summer, autumn, and winter seasons affected me differently as I listened and understood what they would reveal. I sensed when rain, thunder or lightning was coming by feeling the Earth and having Spirit visions.

A wonderful thing about growing up in Inverness was being surrounded by fairy hills and ancient magical sites. One of the most beautiful cemeteries in the world is a place called Tomnahurich atop one of the fairy hills. I often went up there to play with my friends in the worlds of Spirit and Nature, including fairies, elementals, and divas who all danced happily together in the sunlight. I collected caterpillars from there, and took great care to raise them into butterflies before releasing them on the hill to fly away with the fairies. I also visited the Clootie Well and the standing stones around the land where I lived. I remember my happiness when playing there.

When I entered secondary school, I found no one with whom I could talk that had gifts like mine. Nor were there any books to help me even if I had the patience to read. Then on a rare day when I was not playing truant I overheard friends talking about visiting the Highland Seer. I asked them if I could come along, and with their parents we set out a few days later for the house where Swain McDonald was giving readings that week. I can see the street in Inverness even to this day. He was at 9 Union Road and the house still stands. I went inside and saw a man who looked so very much like the sage and magician with his long hair and white beard.

Swain came from a hereditary craft family that worked with the land traditionally. His seership lineage went back to ancestors who fought in the Battle of Culloden. Swain had already traveled the world, and as he sat communicating with Spirit I just knew that here was someone who understood with a great passion what I knew. I remember vividly when he first looked at me and said that I had his gift of second sight. He immediately encouraged my mastery of having and interpreting visions and dreams through scrying and other ancient ways. I really had found someone who understood who I was.

The Black Isle in the Highlands of Scotland is where Kenneth McKenzie died, and where many other seers throughout the ages have lived. Swain made his permanent home on the Black Isle. I visited his croft there as often as possible, usually in the company of other people and friends because of my age. His magnificent sitting room had all the amazing things I could imagine seeing in a wizard's room.

During this time of my life, I started seeing a shamanic double. It was very strange to walk along and see myself in front of me. I was glad that Swain was around to explain these things. When I joined Swain for walks on the land, we would listen to Spirit and Nature to develop my gifts and abilities. He repeated for me the advice of the ancient ones: intuition is the key to initiation. We went out one night to Glen Urquart Castle at Loch Ness and saw Spirit orbs floating above the grass and flying around. It was amazing.

Shortly after I left home at the age of fifteen, a dear woman called Mrs. Fraser took me to the spiritualist church. This is where and when I started developing my mediumship abilities. One night I was slouched in my seat at the very back of a hall in Inverness when the woman who was the medium that evening turned in my direction from the platform. She told me that she knew I was trying to hide, but the Spirit world insisted that she tell me to develop my gifts and abilities, and that one day I would become a famous medium.

I went through a wild phase of teenage rebellion, especially against school and all the restrictions that were placed upon me there. I did not want to learn what I was being taught, yet I was willing to try to fit in with society. It is very difficult to walk the seership path alone, and living on my own in Inverness as a teenager was difficult indeed. However, I found acceptance from the people who attended the meetings at the spiritualist church. I was relieved that Swain and I were not the only ones constantly communicating with Spirit.

Swain McDonald had such a great love of Spirit. He did amazing deeds, had many visions, and helped many people to see their future and shape it. However, Swain was often criticized and judged by people who did not understand his gifts. He did find it difficult to live his life in complete balance. One day about ten years ago and a few years before his debilitating death from alcoholism, I was studying his scrying stone with water in it, the one used by his ancestors back in the times of Kenneth

Mackenzie. He reached over and placed the sacred stone in my hands, saying it was my time to teach and to walk the path of the Highland Seer. With a simple ceremony, he handed on his hereditary title to me. Swain passed into the Spirit world a couple of years ago, yet he continues to weave in and out of my life.

I began to realize that my experiences were taking me beyond the beginning of world history. I became a seer by merging my visions with all the ancient arts, which are divvied up today in my homeland among the Pagan, Wicca, and Druid traditions. My tradition is the oldest, working directly with the earth, air, fire, and water elements without while summoning forth Spirit wisdom from within. Mother Earth shared her bounty with me in every stone I picked up from the land and streams. I peered into crystals and stones to see many things that were going to happen. I knew I was one with Heaven and Nature. It was just this heartless world that upset me.

My spirit grew in power as I reintegrated the ancient wisdom. I recalled that as a little girl I could remember when I first came into this world as well as before this lifetime. I discovered that I more easily developed my seership abilities when my mind and body melted as one in my heart. My soul remembrance developed rapidly as I focused on who I am and what I was feeling. I learnt of the upper and lower worlds through imagination, intuition, inspiration, instinct, miracles and magic. The ancient wisdom from above and below permeated my ideas, feelings, will, and dreams.

Seers journey back to the very beginning of time and are willing to track time forward from the first ancestors. We remember our experiences as ancient Egyptians in the mystery schools, as ancient Indians, Persians, Greeks, Romans, and Native Americans. Long ago, oracles, prophets, and seers lived for hundreds of years on Earth. We stepped out of time, no longer controlled by it. Those of us who deeply felt Nature's power initiated others into Her seeming mysteries. These rites were teachings of the heart through souls and spirits directly from God and the Goddess.

Love was and is the key to maintaining clear channels for the divine mysteries. We become hollow so the love of our hearts will flow through us into the world.

Seers' divine and natural gifts are the abilities of the spirit medium and the natural healer. Myths of goddesses and gods are remnants of the supernatural powers that all humanity once possessed. Gradually the great open traditions of the Goddess and God became concealed within the mystery schools and guarded with the greatest possible secrecy. Violations of the sanctity of these secrets were punishable by death from the guardians themselves.

What is it about this hidden knowledge that prompts even its guardians to fear so much? Why have thousands of us been silenced and kept from remembering who we are and where we have come from, and have suffered death of the body for our inquiries? The answer is nothing less than that we are divine and are from beyond the stars. We remember our connection to the lost tribes of Eden. We listen to the wisdom of these ancestors to avoid repeating our mistakes.

Today, shamans continue to travel into the other worlds of our one reality. This is why shamanism is akin to seership. Yet even some shamans have diluted their powers by specializing as psychics and healers, or concentrating on past-life therapies or soul retrievals. They reveal only in part our heart's gifts. Similarly, our mind's reasoning is only part of our whole-minded nature. Practical minds learn of traditions once personally remembered by clear seeing, and then passed on by word of mouth before writing took form. Writing forces us to think, which is not the same as using our abilities of inspired knowing and natural remembrance.

With grace, we release our limited beliefs and unnatural fears. We trust again our all-knowing and one-feeling heart. This is a big leap from relying on what we have learnt through the world. When I listen to different medicine men and wise women from around the world, they remind me how to bring forth from within the wisdom and love of Heaven and Nature. True knowledge is instinctive. Trusting our intuitions is natural. When we remember our only beautiful feeling, called true love, bliss, or compassion, we readily see into the other worlds of our one reality. We evolve our human nature and create our divine destiny.

Is the world ready again for such self-discovery and unworldly responsibility? Seers, prophets, and mystics are still condemned in one way or another. Will the persecution stop only when the wisdom carriers are no longer? Will seers become myths like unicorns and Pegasus? Will Jesus disappear like Atlantis from our collective consciousness? By the time of the Bible writings, God was already lamenting that His prophets and seers were ignored and slain.

Divine messengers continue to reveal our pasts and futures, as natural and supernatural record keepers at sacred sites and in sacred spaces throughout the world. Today, a road slices through both Delphi in Greece and Avebury in Britain. At Stonehenge, an underpass is under consideration. These actions reflect the will of selves to separate from the One will.

It is time to integrate all the information from this chapter into your personal story. In the following exercise, we will build an altar to your ancestors. We will use objects from your own homelands and your own journeys to connect you to where you have come from. This is the first of our ten exercises, so it is both a foundation and an overview of the seership gifts and abilities which you will unveil and practice as we further explore the worlds of selves, spirits, and souls.

Exercise 1   HONOURING OUR ANCESTORS

Many traditions honour the memory of their dead. Loved ones have slept near their dead, and ancient Celts and Egyptians even lived for a time in the cemeteries of their departed to maintain a closer connection. In much of Africa and parts of Asia an ancestral altar is the sacred centre of the home. It continues to be the focal point for contacting the Spirit world in the Druid and Voodoo traditions. For Native Americans the ancestral altar was part of their everyday life, keeping alive the memory of those who had already completed their Earth walk.

Ancestors are those who gave birth to us or raised us in this lifetime, as well as their parents before them. Ancestors are also of the land where you live today. For example, if you are of Irish descent living in America you would honour both your Irish blood ancestors and the stewards of the American land where you make your home.

When you look around your home you may find that you already have an ancestral altar but do not realise it. Where are the photos of your loved ones who have passed to the Spirit world? Are candles already there? We form a bridge, a communication link, to spirits of the people in our life we have loved and seemingly lost when we create a special place for the photos, flowers, jewellery, and other items that remind us of them. An ancestral altar keeps them near you. You can use the altar to be your own seer, connecting directly with the departed and sensing their presence.

Many people have asked me during their readings to help them with the problem of where to put their ancestor's ashes. Often the ashes are still in urns, and the urns are in the shed or in a cupboard. I know that when these relatives were alive and in their bodies they would not have been happy sitting in a shed or cupboard. Does it not occur to the loved ones that the slamming of the shed door or the rattling of the cupboard dishes might be the ancestor's way of getting their attention? Until a family decides where the final resting place will be for their deceased, it is best to create an ancestral altar and place the urn in the centre.

Let us now build your ancestral altar or complete the one you may have already started. You will need a table if possible. However, if you have altars in every room as I do, space may be limited. Even a section on a shelf is okay because it is your intention that matters. Your altar will be a personalized tribute expressed through the natural elements of fire, water, air, and earth, and the supernatural element of Spirit. This altar will become an external symbol of your inner heart space. The sacred space reflects your natural connection with divinity, without as within, below as above.

Choose a wonderful covering or cloth for your altar. I find spirits love colour, so make it bright unless you prefer a more reverent theme of white or black. At special times of the year, such as your ancestor's birthday or anniversary, you may want to change colours. I find the connection very powerful when I do a ceremony on an anniversary or birthday of an ancestor's passing.

What persons, places, and things did your ancestor love? Place pictures or mementos of these on the altar. Then arrange the flowers and jewellery they most adored. You may even want to include a morsel of the foods or sweets they enjoyed, especially chocolates.

Use one or more candles to represent the element of fire. In nearly all cultures and religions, past and present, candles or small dishes of nut oils burn to invoke the Spirit world. Use a clay vessel or other safe container. The candle colour is up to you. One of the purposes of this exercise is to remove your uncertainty about the "correct" way to honour your ancestors. Ask Spirit directly when you become confused by details like colour. With Spirit's help, you remember to create and recreate, enjoy miracles and magic, and trust your intuitions and instincts.

A small bowl of water on the altar is next. To personalize this offering, consider the water reference you most associate with your ancestor's spiritual practices or activities in Nature. For example, if they led a Christian life then holy water from their parish church is a wonderful tribute. If their religion is not what resonates with your memory of them, obtain your water from a special place like the Chalice Well in Glastonbury, England, or from a mountain stream, river, or sea that had significance for your ancestor.

The element of air is represented at your altar from the smoke of sacred sage, cedar, frankincense, or other incenses of your choice. When you burn these fragrant offerings in memory of your ancestors, the smoke will help you visualize the rising of your prayers heavenward. Buy pure and natural incense, or use herbs or resins from the land that your ancestors would have used for their own sacred ceremonies.

Remember as children how we used to play in the earth, how we enjoyed getting dirty as we connected to the land? For the element of earth on your altar, if possible go to the land of your ancestor's birth and collect some soil. Otherwise, some earth from where you were born will do just fine. On my altar, I have soil from Scotland to honour my parents and their parents. For our ancestors and ourselves it helps when we have ventured away from home to have a bit of earth from where we come, just like Count Dracula. However, you do not need to have a coffin full of soil. Just a jar is enough.

The element of Spirit is our actual connection to our ancestors. Natural beings have spirits in common forever. When we place our intention to connect with our ancestors while in the sacred space of an altar, the Spirit world feels welcomed to manifest into this reality. We honour our ancestors when we call out their names, pray to them to help us heal our hurts and pains, and ask them for forgiveness.

When you are ready to hear and feel your ancestor's response to your call, you will find that they want above all to ask forgiveness from you. They are sorry for the suffering they may have caused by not fully appreciating and understanding you. I am still amazed when doing readings that so many ancestors come through and ask for forgiveness from their family. They now understand love and wish to communicate their deep regret for the times when they were alive that they acted unloving. Working with your ancestral altar will heal your issues of yesterday so you can be complete and whole today.

Now that your altar is ready, it is time for your connection to the world of ancestors. Consider taking the rest of the day off to reflect upon what you receive from Spirit. Ensure that no one will disturb you during ceremony in your sacred space. Switch off electronics in hearing range and place courtesy signs on doors.

Light your incense, sage, or herbs and walk around the room in whatever way feels right for you to create a sacred space. This purification or smudging is how we use the element of air. Light your candle to invoke the element of fire. Then take the earth in your hand and in your own way bring to mind that we all come from the Earth and to the Earth we will return.

Next, take the water and ask to be washed clean of all pains, hurts, and fears that have stopped you from connecting with your loved ones. Place all the thoughts and feelings that no longer serve your highest good into the water. Feel the energy of forgiveness wash them away. By healing past hurts and pains, we move forward to a new and deeper understanding of our heritage and our birthright. We heal through prayers sent to Heaven on the wings of forgiveness.

You are now ready to call forth your ancestor's spirits. Our connection to Spirit is prayer and intention. We ask to receive. Say, "I call forward now my ancestors, my grandmothers and grandfathers, to be with me here in this sacred space. I am here to listen to you. I am asking for your guidance and help." Call out the names of those you wish to contact. Invite them to be with you in your sacred space. Take the time to connect to your ancestors and thank them for their understanding and wisdom. Ask them for assistance in cleansing your memories until only the beauty of the past remains. Ask for their guidance in all present difficulties. Ask them to bless you with what they see as your bright future.

When you feel that you have completed a healing for both yourself and your ancestral family, thank your ancestors for coming and being with you in your sacred space. Feel how lovely your life seems now that you have closure. Let the candle burn down, and use the ceremonial water to nurture a special plant in your garden or house. As it grows, allow this plant to remind you of your earthly bond with Nature and your ancestral bond with Heaven.

CHAPTER 2

LOVING OURSELVES

I tell a story when I am running workshops and it is amazing the response I get. It is a story of a beautiful little girl who is born into this world out of the love of her parents. They exclaim, "What a beautiful child! We love you. We will take care of you and nurture you. We will be there for you no matter what. We accept you just the way you are." This child grows up in a caring environment with brothers and sisters who love her because they see themselves in her.

When it is time for school, to the child's delight she is met at the school gate by her teacher who says, "I will be there for you. Whatever you wish to learn I will help you to achieve it. We will help you learn the left-brained way and the right-brained way, always to support the development of your natural abilities." The child grows up with love because her parents and teachers want the best for her and encourage her dreams of becoming whatever she wants to be.

Her parents take her to church, where they listen to stories about all the different religions to gain a deeper understanding of how we are connected by Spirit throughout the world's history. She finishes with the schools and begins the work she has dreamt of doing. She enjoys her workplace and the people there. She feels happy and complete. Then she meets the man or woman of her dreams. She knows she has found her soul mate.

They get married and soon desire to share their great love by having a child of their own. The ideal human love cycle begins again. When I tell this story in front of 100 people and ask how many of them have lived this life, one or two at the most will raise their hands. Sad but true.

We look at young children and see their inner gifts of wisdom and joy. Children remind us of our connection with the Spirit world, as wonderfully told in the well-known report of a little boy who wanted to speak with his newborn baby sister. This true story includes the parents' initial interference with his nursery visit, reflecting society's discouragement of our natural curiosity. What did the little boy say to his littler sister? "Please remind me where I've come from before I totally forget who I am."

We are born knowing love from past experiences. We come to this Earth as innocent children with memories of our interconnectedness. When I came into this lifetime, I wished to love so much. I remember as a little girl my mother opening the front door to gypsies and other strangers. I would put my arms around them and hug them and my parents would wonder how I could love these people.

As much as possible I lived my early childhood with Spirit and in Nature, not in the world of growing up. I remember once lying on the floor and my parents saying to me, "you are a strange child, this is not how we brought you up." I gained knowledge through visions of places like the Native American lands, and got upset by watching the television when the cowboys always won. I would cry over the Native American deaths, and when my parents asked me why I was crying I told them the truth. I had been there and those native people were my kin.

My parents told me not to be so silly and that it was just my imagination. I wonder how many of us were told the same discouraging words. I went back to my room and sat there in the dark, telling myself that Spirit was not real and that spirits were just figments of my imagination. The Spirit world turned to me and gently assured me that the world of my parents, the schools and church was a mere shadow of Heaven and Nature.

Spirit again gave me the courage to trust my imagination no matter what. It is easy for Spirit to visit with us when we are children because the outer world has not yet fully erected its gatekeepers on our inner sensing. Spirit made me gleefully expectant of doors opening, people walking through walls and sitting on the edge of my bed, and other wondrous signs.

I followed where Spirit led me. I knew of no other way, as my Spirit family was kind, loving and caring. There was never a cross word from Spirit and my Spirit family was always there for me. At times, I would cry my eyes out because my parents did not understand me. They had issues of their own, always seemed to be arguing, and I was determined not to get involved in this.

When I was still five years old I went outside one night, looked at the stars, and pointing upwards I asked to go Home. I did not want to be in a world where no one understood or wanted me. Spirit just laughed and said the problem was my imagination was running away from me. They made me feel so proud to be a child of the stars. I wanted to please Spirit in return by playing in the world some more. I welcomed back my imagi-nation and let it run away with me.

Many parental practices continue the loveless customs dating from at least biblical times and modified in the socially repressive Victorian era. I remember, "Please may I leave the table?" while sitting with adults and wanting to play or get away from the boring conversations. The belief was that children should be seen and not heard, and that a child must be controlled by crushing her spirit. This appalling way of parenting still is practiced today. Egyptian children judged too difficult to control are taken to the sheik to remove their spirit, their natural wilfulness and life force.

Loving parents know how to love themselves. My parents grew up during the Second World War. They survived one day at a time, afraid to love another in case they lost that loved one to the horror of war. Parents who do not know their own infinite worth pass on to us what they have learnt from their hardships, failures, and fears. My father was a chartered accountant, so he insisted that I was brought up learning the academic ways.

The problem was that the schools offered little of interest to me, and my gifts of being psychic, dyslexic, left-handed, creative, and willful were not valued within or without my home. At school I was stigmatized for my dyslexia and beaten across my knuckles for writing with my left hand. My father sympathized with my plight, but did not interfere. When younger he was forced to write with his right hand because his teachers strapped his left hand behind his back.

As a girl, I loved going to ballet class, an experience that was easy for my inner mind's creative nature. I also attended piano lessons, although this was more challenging for my outer mind's thinking nature. I excelled at ballet but not at piano. My mother gave me an ultimatum to either study harder at piano which I was hopeless at because I could not consistently read the music, or give up ballet. Since the piano teacher said I was a difficult child and would never learn music, my mother barred me from continuing what I most loved, practicing ballet.

In those days, there was not yet a correct understanding of the distinction between learning differences and learning difficulties. Like many seers, I am blessed with gifts of sensitivity rather than the more readily measurable quantitative skills. I was consistently told by my schoolteachers that I was stupid, which they cruelly reinforced with terrible beatings and unrestricted humiliation. Yet I shined in every sport I participated in that got me out of the classroom. I loved running, swimming, cycling, and ball playing because I did not have to think and I was out in Nature.

My mother belted me relentlessly for having the courage to follow my heart's natural desires and wisdom. She said I could only please her if I was as good at my schoolwork as I was in sports. If only she understood my great gifts. I wish there had been schools to develop and encourage my natural gifts and abilities. How much more suffering will creative and spiritually gifted children have to endure before our minority is socially accepted and nurtured?

Dyslexic people challenge an academic system designed to develop, measure, and report on the practical, analytic, and logical features of the brain. Our society and our schools give minimum appreciation to our psychic and creative gifts as it is easier to judge and reward reading, writing, and mathematical skills. Because we are an almost insignificant statistic in society in general and to the budget conscious schools in particular, dyslexics continue to be undereducated and our cleverness remains undervalued.

Long before I knew what dyslexia meant, I asked Spirit why I had this burden. They replied that dyslexia is actually a way for us not to rely on reading other people's words. Instead, we could more easily hear the words that come to us directly from our hearts. Spirit also said that because of this gift, I would be able to speak of my experiences to many others using the simple words from my heart. My Spirit family acknowledged my imagination and implored me to recognize that all the wondrous visions I saw with my child's inner sight were and are real.

A thin thread of conscious child development practices weaves its way today among a few primary schools, which encourage at a minimum our wise childish ways of sharing milk and cookies, holding hands when skipping down a lane, and napping comfortably in each other's laps. There are even rarer secondary schools and universities that nurture the gifted and creative in a more natural way.

For the many of us to whom the experience of ideal childhood nurturing and education was denied or curtailed, we must still clear our inner child hurts and pains before working effortlessly from our hearts as seers. We complete our needless journey away from Spirit and our souls by coming home again to our inner child's wisdom and wellness. We avail our awareness and compassion to Heaven and Nature's service and learn to distinguish true from false among thoughts and feelings that are ours, those of the person we are giving a reading to and those that we sense belong to the Spirit world's messengers.

When it came time for attending church I assumed I was being taken to learn what loving people knew about the heart worlds. Immediately I could not understand why there was only a male God. Where was the female? When I asked I was told women were sinful and that we were evil and bad. They declared there was no Goddess, only a loving, kind and gentle God.

If He is so loving, kind, and gentle then why did he not love women? My questions disturbed the benumbed churchgoers. I knew because of my experiences that Spirit was never judgmental. Nor does Spirit place fear or shame into our hearts. I was told in the supposed house of God that I was the child of the devil because I saw spirits. These churchgoing people placed upon me their shame, fear and guilt. How could this be? I was very confused.

My childhood experiences in this world bore out that my parents, the schools and the church did not teach how to love unconditionally. Nor did they teach initiation rites and rites of passage because they do not remember them. It is lost wisdom, the knowledge no longer allowed to us. We are only taught what everyone except us has decided we need to know about the world.

We can make life easier for everyone by changing our present relationship with ourselves and not allowing our past conditioning to influence future generations. Where are our rites of passage for girls to honour their sudden ability to bear children? When I came into my womanhood I was told it was a curse. Where did that lack of wisdom come from? Where are the training and initiation rites for boys to become real and gentle men? Ancient and indigenous cultures honoured this passage, why does our western society not?

Instead of significant rites, we were given false beliefs about our purpose in life. The real meaning of life was hidden from us and replaced with man made ideas of economics, warfare, and hell. We can begin to change our world's loveless structure by choosing today to lay our own fear-based reactions to rest. As children we learnt to survive, but by doing so we hid away our souls within our hearts.

We have been conditioned since childhood to tolerate a life without passion, Spirit, and true meaning. We were forced by the world to sacrifice our hearts to our selves. Selves continue to react to their childhood suffering by their present lack of self worth. They judge themselves and others and linger in states of fear, shame, and guilt. Selves feel unworthy of deep healing love because the world's teachings and teachers have stolen away our hearts.

We can become strong enough to heal our emotional wounds by remembering that the self-judgments we carry with us are not our true knowledge of our blessed innocence. We can refuse to listen to the echoes of our false nurturers who told us we are bad and wrong. This is not the real you. It is the conditioned you. It is your self.

Once, when I was feeling sad, a dear friend of mine told me to get off my cross because we needed the wood. We really do not need to suffer for sins of selves anymore. I remember as a small child sitting on my father's knee saying, "Its okay daddy, I will make you better." He was an alcoholic and workaholic, and I truly believed that I could take away all his pain and hurt. When he died, I blamed myself.

As children, we feel responsible for whatever happens to us. I condemned myself for my father's death and my mother's frustration. I felt responsible for all the upset in the family. My mother told me I was bad, so I told myself I was unloved and unworthy.

When I left home I continued to believe I was no good, an idiot and a child of the devil because this was drummed into me by my family, school and church. What chance did I have in the world to do the good I knew of when those around me were telling me these lies? I was only a child in years, yet I was hopelessly holding on to all the negative emotions of other people's judgments. I carried this burden around with me for a very long time.

With Swain's help, I started to understand that I was not at fault. I had yet to re-learn that being responsible is not the same as blaming me. I kept suppressing my emotions, feeling ashamed about my reactions to situations and allowing my childhood wounds to control my life. I was my own worst enemy.

We begin to understand what happened to the beautiful child that was crushed and forgotten when we see the effect it has had on us as adults. We open our hearts again to sing of our true worth and loveliness. We are ready for healing. We forgive the many in our lives that controlled our destiny while knowing not what they were doing. We forgive ourselves for believing in what we knew did not ring true to our hearts.

It is time to step back into the Garden of Eden that we have never really left. Our all-knowing and all-loving hearts have been here all this time waiting for us to remember that we are not lost souls or forgotten spirits. We still feel the heartbeat of our Great Mother Earth. We are as we were born, children of Nature with empty hands bearing Heaven's treasures. Our child body's infinite gaze is our soul's sensing, our fresh insight, and our seer's vision.

Our physical eyes are released from the outer world when we look within. This is the "far away" look of children, artists, mystics and seers. Seers stay young in heart and soul while maturing in mind, body, and Spirit. Seers remember and honour our inner child. As children, we looked in vain outside ourselves for answers to what we never questioned before our own inner guidance was hushed up by the world. Yet we remain forever worthy to receive the divine love and knowing that resides in our hearts.

The forbidden knowledge is our heart's wisdom. We become our own teacher again and re-learn to trust the power within us. Our souls are the Holy Grail that we have been seeking for thousands of years outside ourselves. Recall the ancient story wherein the wise ones asked, "Where is the last place on Earth that humans would think to look for the true knowledge?" "I know," said one, "let us hide it within their hearts because they would never think to look there."

Many people come to me for readings and I will ask them after a while why they are not listening. Not to me but to their inner voice, the internal wisdom and wealth that patiently awaits our attention. I remember once my mother asking me why I had to learn the hard way. My reply was that when I follow my knowing will, I fully experience what I need to learn.

I try to experience at least once in this lifetime as much as I possibly can. I feel there is no point in reaching 80, 90 or 100 years old and wishing I had experienced more. My will follows the ancient wisdom of not leaving to tomorrow what I can experience today. When we postpone experience, we simultaneously make a reservation at the place of regrets. Seers and children know how to live without regrets. By being happy and compassionate during our Earth walk, we see the Earth again through the knowing eyes of the innocent children we still are.

Seers make a simple choice to awaken in this lifetime from who we are not. We live our joy. We let another experience their joy. We often join in another's joy. Usually, we offer to share our joy with another because we get such pleasure from within that sharing it merely increases our joy, never diminishing it. Notice how children are ever ready to share their joy by playing, until this enthusiasm is made wrong.

When we ask from whom we learnt about love, we realize how many of them were carrying unhealed wounds within themselves that they burdened on us. Look at how others' hurts that you have taken as yours are affecting you today. Are you still acting out the victim? I was when I met James. My tumultuous relationship with him was the turning point in my life, for it helped me see who I was not.

He pushed all my buttons and showed me the beautiful child beneath the hurt and pain inflicted by others, and the lack of worth and love I felt for myself. When this life lesson was complete and I was whole, we released each other, for he was now the mirror that no longer could hold my healed reflection. I thank James for helping me to see again the star child that Spirit knows me to be.

During the dramas of my life when I was not listening to my soul, my Spirit family never deserted me. As I write these words I am celebrating my 50th birthday, and to me that is 50 years of amazing experiences. My odysseys of heart-discovery have left me wiser and grateful. I feel well now. I have rid myself of past attachments and I trust that I am prepared for the exciting times ahead of us on Earth.

Our worldly seeking becomes purposeful when it readies us to under-stand who we are not. We grow up, marry, have families and then we get to the age of about 40 or 50 and our children have grown up and left home. All of a sudden we look at our selves and feel lost. We call this the mid-life crisis. We stop being the daughter or the son, the brother or the sister, and the mother or the father. We stop being ourselves.

Things just seem to happen at mid-life because we begin to wake up from who we are not and for the first time in our lives we are stuck or lost and do not know what we want or who we are. From our birth, we are not taught who we are. At mid-life, we have another opportunity to listen to our inner voice and see with our inner eyes. We meet again our inner child at the suspended place of our last encounter.

Long-held grievances are useful clues for disclosing how our inner child is still feeling victimized. We can gather the courage to release the mental and emotional traumas of our inner child that our adult selves still suffer from. We can empower our souls as adults by correcting the foolish and harmful lessons we were taught as children. We update our role models from those that never or no longer serve our spiritual development to those who resonate with our passion and purpose.

My desire as a girl to accommodate my father's behaviour continued to be the model for my relationships long after I left his house. I believed that I had to put up with men who were abusive, absent, drunk and unfaithful to be worthy of their partnership. I attracted relationship after relationship with these clones of my father. If I chanced to meet a good and kind man, I could not accept that I was actually worthy of his love.

I was still playing out the daughter-father role when I met James. I experienced strong emotional reactions to what he said and did. My enraged, injured and frightened inner child wanted desperately to be seen and heard. I was ready as if for the first time in my life to love this familiar yet dreadful victim of such utter innocence. I was willing to honour her and comfort her and finally to bring about a sacred union with my inner soul and outer self.

It is not easy for many of us to listen to the inner voice that speaks of loving ourselves. When I lead heart-to-heart workshops I get people to hug each other. Many people are uncomfortable with hugging, and otherwise find it difficult to express their hearts. I joke about the British with their stiff upper lip before asking those having difficulty if they are ready to love and respect themselves. Until we cherish our hearts we are fooling ourselves and others, especially if we are practitioners of the healing arts. Unhealed healers can still be helpful towards others who are more desperate for love than they are. Healings that are miracles are available to all who serve Great Spirit and have accepted the grace of our Great Mother's divine love for us.

To feel this grace, many seers have undergone great learning experiences of life and love. When someone comes to a seer because a family member joined the Spirit world, the seer who has also grieved over the passing of a loved one can effectively help the bereaved. Seers comfort those who are in anguish from their loss by letting them know their loved one is still with them. Spirits use the seer's personal emotional experiences to form a heartfelt connection between the living and their deceased.

We all have wonderful love within us. Love is like a seed. It is planted in the innermost core of our very being. We nurture this seed until it grows and fills our hearts. We become the essence, the lotus flower, the bud of all life. By sowing our seeds of love, we redevelop our conscious connection with our hearts. The greater our love the greater will be the creative force of the future and our destiny. From love will grow the spiritualisation of the Earth. The more spiritual knowledge and joy that flow from our hearts into our minds and bodies, the more we evolve into whole and well human beings.

Exercise 2   LOVING OURSELVES

Seers know the immeasurable value of love. Love comes to us from within and without. We feel, see, thank, and trust our sacredness. We deeply love ourselves and experience deeply loving relationships with others. Our compassionate hearts and joyous souls beckon others to respond in kind. The mate to our soul, the twin of our passions, hears our silent call and answers.

The sacred knows us as beautiful, wonderful, and innocent. We are the beloved of our hearts. Do you love yourself completely as Spirit does? Do you live from your all-seeing soul and all-knowing heart? Do you value yourself, cherish yourself, and praise yourself? One way to remember the answer to "who am I?" is by experiencing the honour of your heart in a sacred marriage to yourself.

Sacred marriage rituals are from prehistoric times. These ceremonies bring abundance and fertility to the land and its people by honouring the unions of Heaven and Nature, God and Goddess, male and female, body and soul, mind and Spirit, hearts and Heart.

For the Sumerians the sacred marriage was an important royal ritual of feasting and celebration. The King led the procession to the Goddess Inanna's temple. The sacred union of the divine masculine and feminine was represented by the ritualised sexual union of the King and either the Queen or the High Priestess. First Nation Native Americans believed that long ago man and woman were one before separating. Since that day, we have all been searching for our split-apart to re-experience our remembered wholeness. In the Sophia tradition of Gnostic Christianity, Jesus' teachings honoured and balanced the divine masculine and feminine. Divine illumination is achieved through the sacred union of the male and female principles within oneself.

My sacred marriage took place in the small temple of Amun in Karnak, Egypt. Within this beautiful temple stands a statue of the Goddess Sekhmet. She is the lion-headed goddess of magic and healing, and a protector of both the living and the dead. I came to Sekhmet because I was ready to let go of all my inner child wounds. James was the catalyst of this healing of my inner child, and I was ready to let go and love myself unconditionally.

As I stood in this sacred place before Sekhmet with my friend and witness Patricia, I wondered how many others like us over the thousands of years had come to this goddess with offerings. I lit a candle between her feet, placed the flowers around her and burnt kyphi, an ancient mix of Egyptian incenses, as an offering of gratitude for allowing me to be in this sacred place undisturbed.

We could feel the love and passion emanating from the Goddess as I spoke the words: "I will honour, love, respect, and care for myself. I will listen to my beautiful inner child's wants and needs. She is loved once again." I could feel a change, an initiation into a new understanding and being. By coming to this sacred place of the Goddess I was showing the world of Spirit I was ready in my life for cosmic change to take place. I was changing my perception of my own self-image. I was getting rid of all the negative beliefs that I had held in my life.

I saw my whole life flash in front of me during those few seconds. I then vowed in front of Sekhmet that I would help others see the beauty and feel the power of true love. For the first time in my life I felt complete. I could feel my soul and heart as one with Spirit, as I remember feeling from childhood. Now my mind and body joined in the sacred union. I returned to wholeness and well-being.

Patricia stood beside me the entire time. At the end of the ceremony, she was so moved by what happened to me that she asked Sekhmet to help release her neglected pains and clinging fears. We finished her ceremony, honoured the Goddess, left the sacred site and thanked the Egyptian temple guardians who had ensured our privacy.

Once outside Patricia experienced feeling very ill. This was clearing energy, moving and changing her from inside out. It worked. By the end of the day Patricia too was feeling whole, complete and renewed.

For your sacred marriage to yourself, choose a date, a time and a sacred place. Your sacred place may be at home by yourself or with friends. It may be in Nature at a sacred grove, spring or other site, wherever you can fully celebrate with music, dance, song, food and wine if you choose. It is totally up to you. It is your wedding day.

You will need a special ring to commemorate this joyous day, perhaps an old one passed on to you by your grandparents or a newly made one of your unique design. I bought in Egypt a gold ring depicting Isis, the ancient goddess of magic and healing. She is also a protector of permanent love commitments, which of course includes our eternal relationship with Spirit in our hearts.

Compose the words that you will say to yourself, or you may feel that the inspiration will come later to speak directly from your heart. Select the candles, flowers, music, food, wine, and whatever else feels appropriate for your special occasion. Have colours in your space that reflect your feelings. Pink suggests love, green represents life, and white evokes innocence.

Prepare your body on the morning of your chosen day by enjoying either a long soak in the bath with lots of bubbles, candles, and soft music, or a cleansing shower during which you take time to feel the element of water washing over you. Next, take all your wonderful lotions, potions, oils and scents and anoint yourself as has been done since ancient times. Remember the power of your childhood imagination and become a king preparing himself for his queen, or the high priestess readying herself for the mysteries of the night. Let your imagination run away with you.

Adorn yourself with your finest robes or special occasion clothing. Experience how good it feels dressing up for a big date with you. Final touches are make-up and jewellery if desired. You are ready to look in the mirror and welcome back your inner beauty. See through the eyes of a child once again, and remember who you are. Have fun, laugh; it is your special day.

When you arrive at your sacred place you may want to have your favourite music playing. Become mindful of the presence of the divine in your midst, and cleanse the room or area with sage or incense as an invitation to the Spirit world to witness your ceremony. Light your candle. Offer your special prayer or invocation to your guides and loved ones in the Spirit world to be with you, as they are ever ready to do.

You are ready to speak the words of your affirmation to your heart.

These are your sacred love vows, sending a powerful message into all worlds of your total and unconditional love for you. It is a powerful experience to use a mirror as you say these words directly from your heart to your heart. Be gentle with yourself in this moment.

Place the ring on your wedding ring finger. This finger connects with your heart along its meridian line. Your mind, body, soul and spirit rejoin and rejoice in the bond of eternal honour and care of your heart.

When the sacred moment of reunion is complete for you, celebrate however you wish with friends or family or on your own. Well done. Be very proud of yourself. Honour yourself. Love yourself. I leave you with the words of a beautiful song that reminds me of the Great and Holy Spirit's unconditional love:

I will be gentle with myself,
I will love myself,
I am a child of the universe being born each moment.
I will be gentle with myself,
I will heal myself,
I am a child of the universe being born each moment.

CHAPTER 3

HEALING OURSELVES

Long before Jesus' Earth walk, the Greek seer and philosopher Socrates said "The cure of the part should not be attempted without treatment of the whole. No attempt should be made to cure the body without the soul. Let no one persuade you to cure the mind until he has first given you his spirit. For the great error of our day is that physicians separate the heart from the mind, and the mind from the body."

Wellness is our balanced mind and body. Healing is the art of understanding our mental and physical imbalances and restoring their harmony with our heart. Healing was whole and complete medical treatment in ancient times. Babylonian and other ancient cultures knew the ways of using medicines, prayers and magic. Ancient healers in Tibet and India used sacred breaths of energy. All life is connected by our sacred breaths of energy.

Illness is an imbalance of life energy. Our bodies are sensitive at the cellular and DNA levels to energy disturbances. Seers impartially look into a body and locate these imbalances. We are detached observers because our inner seer's eye does not see death, illness, or incompleteness. We have compassion for others because we have experienced clearing our own energy imbalances. We heal with miracles from our infinitely patient Spirit.

Native cultures of many modern countries still understand these healing ways and use them either solely or to complement available western or allopathic medicines. They trust Nature to provide plants for curing physical illness and trust their seers to prepare their minds for welcoming a cure. Complementary healing is being accepted or re-accepted in hospitals all over the world, and just in time. Today we have hundreds of seemingly different complementary, holistic and alternative ways and medicines available from conventional and traditional practitioners. Allopathic medicine remembers its heritage of the ancient wisdom.

We have glimpses of holistic Greek healing from its appearance in recorded history in 600BC to circa 500AD when its influence faded. The Greeks erected temples and shrines honouring the healing cures, prophecy and medicines of Asclepius, the divine son of the Sun god Apollo. Asclepius was taught the art of herbs, cures and healing by the centaur Chiron, the wounded healer and god of resurrections and reincarnations. Their main healing temple was on the island of Kos, home of Hippocrates. Over three hundred healing shrines existed in many other places across the lands and seas of ancient Greece.

Greeks used hygienic therapy of fresh air, rest, good food, prayer, sun, and sea. Today we call it holidays, a word deriving from when we experienced our resting times as holy days or healing days. Travelers by ship from the vast ancient Middle East rested at these healing shrines for nights, days or weeks depending on the nature of their illnesses. They prepared themselves by sleeping in the temple precincts, drinking and bathing in the sacred springs or wells, consciously fasting, participating in ritual worship and becoming one with their surroundings.

Once their dreams showed them they were ready for healing they invited the priest-physicians to attend their temple sleep or incubation. They prayed together to the god Asclepius to visit in their dreams and heal them or give them visions of how to heal themselves. This ancient healing way came to Greece from Egypt and Mesopotamia. Ancient Egyptian Kemetic medicine and healing had already evolved for perhaps 3,000 years.

Male and female physicians, priests, and magicians were seers who worked with spirits and souls to determine whether an illness was physical, emotional, or mental. These seers weaved between the worlds to know if departed spirits who did not realize their death were causing problems by remaining with a loved one. Ancient Egyptians practiced embalming, surgery, and dentistry, as well as harmonious healings of mind and body. Their purification rites considered the wellness of the whole person, using baths, herbs and plants from Nature, magical spells, prayers and invocations.

Western medicine's founding fathers Hippocrates and Galen acknowledged the Kemetic methods as the keystone for their later Greek understanding and elaboration of healing. Galen dreamt that Asclepius came to him with information on remedies and healings. The Greeks made extensive use of Egyptian medicinal expertise, creating their own schools of learning which influenced the ancient cultures of their empire for centuries to come.

Greeks studied with Egyptian seers at the dream and healing temples of Imhotep at Memphis and Philae. They associated Imhotep with Asclepius, and formed a professional association of healers in Egypt under the patronage of Asclepius. Later Greek sciences emphasized empirical observations and thus separated their earlier holistic wisdom into the supernatural and Nature, the metaphysical and the physical.

Today we have specialist doctors for physical and mental ease, and a similar array of churches, support groups, and televised spiritual workers for emotional and psychic relief. Seers concentrate on emotional and psychic healing since physical and mental healing soon follow. As with doctors of any practical skill, seers often take years to know Spirit's purpose for our psychic gifts and abilities.

I have seen throughout the years an increase in different types of healing. It is amazing that so many people are opening up to the wonderful world of healing, yet it gets very confusing as to which healing we need. I trained in Sekmen Egyptian healing and Reiki healing to understand their differences from the spiritualist and shamanic healing traditions that I practiced. My brain became confused. The answer I was seeking from these outer experiences is to keep healing simple.

Psychic wellness is Spirit healing. Seers harmonize with the Spirit world to assist healing spirits. We step out of the way and welcome Spirit to work through us, allowing the healing energy of life to flow. We do not interfere with the energy. The seer's mind and body are completely consistent with each other and with Spirit during psychic healing.

Seers are open-minded with no attachments to ideas of what has or should happen. We are pure love when conscious of our connection to our divine source. We live our seemingly changing moments as abundant souls expressing Spirit. We travel to the Spirit and natural worlds during psychic and emotional healing. Our methods include inner child release, soul retrieval, and past life resolution. We join with our power animals, Spirit guides and plant spirit medicines when needed to gather our own personal power for assisting in the healing process.

We combine our wisdom and knowledge of ceremony and ritual to clear away old patterns and beliefs no longer needed within our own body and mind. We can then work to make another well by living as examples of wholeness and happiness. Seers connect first with our own hearts, then to the heart of the person being healed. We form a heartfelt bond of compassion and understanding. We then connect with our Spirit guides and helpers, who connect to the other person's Spirit guides and helpers, to form a team of Spirit workers for the healing to take place.

Relations in the Spirit world come forward to assist in the healing of their loved ones on Earth. There can be countless reasons besides issues with the departed for a person who suffers loss of energy to seek healing of psychic or emotional unease. Trauma and abuse in this or a past lifetime, stress, conflict, guilt, negative thinking, serious accidents and relationship break-ups are examples.

To be healed we must want to be well. We let go of fears associated with our illness, and believe we can be healed by trusting Spirit completely. Healing intention is affected by our individual development of personal power, which is a reflection of our beliefs about our selves. When our thoughts and ideas are original, whole and holy we are listening to our divine wisdom and feeling our heart's love. We feel Great Spirit's needless fatherly forgiveness and we heal our minds. We feel the Holy Spirit's needed motherly touch, and we heal our bodies.

Mothers are natural healers who kiss away our hurts and pains. We use our love as a healing energy to focus on making our children well. Love heals where nothing else will work. Actually, love heals as well when other methods succeed. To love ourselves is a healing all of its own. Every one of us has the ability to self-heal, whether we choose to do so or not. All of us are healers. Hugging someone is a healing. Touching someone in our everyday lives makes a difference.

We heal ourselves when we say to someone, "I love you". We heal the world with each loving gesture because every act of kindness connects us with the spirits and souls of all worlds. When we heal our mind by listening to our heart's wisdom we know how to listen to Spirit through other minds. When we heal our body by feeling and seeing it with our heart's love, we know how to sense the souls of other bodies.

I remember Spirit telling me what my food intolerances were while I was in my car driving to the allergy centre. Of course, the tests later confirmed all Spirit told me. Truly listening to our bodies is listening to Spirit speaking through our hearts and souls. During a seership reading one day, Spirit informed me that the other person had a certain allergy. When I told her, she admitted having that very thought repeatedly without acknowledging that it was her body's wisdom.

It has taken me fifty years to slow down and stop running myself into the ground. I am honouring my body while writing and playing in Egypt with rest, sunshine, good food, and spiritual communion, much like the healing we did here thousands of years ago. I am visiting healing temples in Egypt to commemorate my wellness. I am celebrating with heartfelt prayers and home-cooked meals.

In workshops and now in writing, I tell of my healing experiences because this is what I know. My first self-healing in Hawaii last year was beautiful, amazing, and simple. It rebalanced my emotional equilibrium. I was encouraged by the ancient wisdom of the Huna and the compas-sionate Aloha Spirit of my Huna teacher, Nahi. I also sought natural Hawaiian remedies for my physical health, since I was just two weeks into my recovery from major surgery. I was introduced to the juice of the noni fruit that grows wild on tropical islands of the Pacific. I drink a sip of this amazing medicine daily, and it continues to help the healing and maintain the wellness of my body.

Obviously, I was ready for big changes in my life in many ways. I remember sitting on the shoreline of the ocean one morning waiting for the Sun to come up. I had my eyes closed praying for a healing on all levels, when Spirit told me to open my eyes. At that moment a honu, the large and graceful Hawaiian sea turtle, surfaced right in front of me. She looked at me, blew water my way, and promptly disappeared.

I walked back to the beach house where I was staying during my two weeks with Nahi, and found a notice slipped under my door advertising Hawaiian lomilomi massage. The house was owned by an old Hawaiian family, and when I asked one of them about the advertisement, he just smiled and said the honu must have sent this message. I had not mentioned to him my private moment earlier at the ocean. For the next few days, I received these healing massages. Two weeks later I was hiking the Kalalau trail, one of the most challenging and scenic trails of the world, as if I was 30 again.

Despite different names, times and places, seers have harmonious understandings of body, mind, heart, soul and Spirit. Spirit is not limited to or by any body. Everything in the universe contains Spirit yet Spirit is more than the physical universe. Spirits are no things and no bodies as well.

Spirit is in the wind, but not of it. Spirit is in the Earth, but not of Her. Spirit is in the seas but not of them. Spirit is in the Sun, but not of Him. Spirit is energy itself and uses all forms from galaxies to electrons to express life. Spirit brings all into form, holds these forms with love and returns them to no form, no body, and no thing. To the Great and Holy Spirit, there are only perfect transformations.

Spirit never leaves Home, and neither do we. We all are from, in and returning to the world of Spirit. Our spirits and souls renew our hearts.

Centred here is our access to all divine knowing and power. Our heart is always well and healed because here our Spirit family rests alertly. Our souls are Spirit's messengers of happiness, venturing forth on journeys of no distance to share joy with us.

Souls and spirits express heartfelt passions and visionary truths through our bodies and minds while remaining formless and thoughtless as Spirit. Spirit assumes forms of beauty to gift bodies with feelings of love and connectedness. Passion is our body's whole and holy sensing, our divinely human feeling of being alive. Passion is our inner heat, our body's life. Our inner body is our soul, our body in the care of our heart. Here is our dream body of play and emotional wellbeing.

All bodies, from stars and moons to rocks, plants, and animals, sense their relationship to space and each other, which is their connection with Spirit. Life forms on Earth, from plants to animals, experience instinctual, natural, and knowing feelings. Humans have the further resource of intuitive minds. We rise to the height of remembering Heaven when listening to our hearts or fall to the depths of our imagined hells when choosing to accept as reality the world's loveless history and our own hurtful life lessons.

Spirit gifts to our mind are whole and holy thoughts, our inner knowing and inner seeing. Our inner mind is our psychic mind, our mind under the influence of our psychic gifts and Spirit thoughts. Truth and wisdom are effortlessly available to us in our inner minds, even before we think to ask. Spirit has but one all-inclusive knowing. Spirit translates love with infinite patience and perfect understanding to our human minds. We recognize our heart's wisdom as intuitions, insights, and visions.

Our outer minds and bodies know of life only in part. We read newspapers and magazines and think hundreds of discrete yet unrelated thoughts. We look to the skies and assign forms and names to the vast universe, cutting its wondrousness to the quick. Our practical, practicing minds seem to be burdened every moment with choices, but nothing in the universe is needful of worry. No choice is the experience of conceding to the truth and listening to our knowing hearts.

Our mind is what we call the experience of choosing what to believe. We choose to be conscious of original thoughts within our mind, and know. Otherwise, we rely on the world's collective experience of outer events as perceived and remembered by our bodies, and think incompletely and in terms of the past only. Whether we are planning our future or being in the moment, if we are not free from the binds of past traumas then our thoughts are merely projections and extensions of our pasts.

When our minds seek without to know selves, the world and our universe, we find confusion, rejection, and unfriendliness. Our bodies instinctively feel when we are being led astray from life as known to our billion-year-old genes. Our body narrows its senses to ease our mind's turmoil. Our body entrusts the mind with the barest of present moment sensing information. Thus, we are left behind in our pasts, minds adrift and bodies frightened into survivalist behaviours. This is trauma.

Our outer minds and bodies, our selves, suffer when we seek wisdom and love outside our hearts. We suffer because there appears to be nothing lasting outside. We heal by reconnecting with our hearts through our inner pathways. Psychic healing releases our minds to accept mental wellness, as emotional healing prepares our bodies for physical health. Comfort for our body and stillness in our mind are the eternal experiences of our heart's peace.

Seers do not settle for bouts of health in our dying bodies and scheduled meditative moments for our distractible minds. Our intelligent searches for meaning are invitations to Spirit to answer with timeless gifts of inner vision, knowingness and guidance. Our instinctual quest for nurturing is answered with our soul's timely gifts of courage, strength and health.

Children are seers of the inner worlds of body and mind. As happy children we never mind our outer minds and bodies. We trust Nature to regenerate our body's instincts. We play within our body and enjoy heartfelt emotions. We listen to our inner mind and remember our Home.

We allow our soul to play within and without our bodies and let Spirit guide within and without our minds. We trust our outer body to mind itself when our soul dreams without it. We sleep with open seer's eyes. Seers are as happy children again, dreaming day and night.

I remember as a child being able to see into and through the body. It appeared transparent to me, not as a solid form. This seemed quite natural and I told people they looked like walking skeletons. Seers remember how to keep in mind what our physical eyes see while using a soft gaze to glance clairvoyantly into the space occupied by a physical body. We look into a body and see things such as allergies and food intolerances.

I look into the body and actually see the areas where problems are arising. I withdraw my attention from my mind's rational world picture so that I can see a physical body as it is. Seers go beyond what the physical eye sees and our doubting mind believes. We look out from our internal eye and become aware of the impressions of the soul, our heart's body. Powerful sensations of energy arise within, which enable us to see separate organs, muscles, and veins. It is not like peering at a cadaver but more like viewing colourful holographic x-rays.

Seers explain to a person what the person's body is making evident on the inner knowing level, the soul world of instant open communications for all who use inner sensing to perceive. All of us have these gifts and abilities. Seers and children know and use them. Seers extend our personal wisdom and experience of the child's inner worlds by integrating them with our mature mind and body faculties in a helpful and comple-mentary way.

Ours is the way of the Heart, the path of least resistance, the road out of nowhere into now here. Our heart communicates via our brain to our mind and body. Heart talk, visions and feelings are detectable in areas of the brain but these measurements are the shadows of our inner sensing, ripples in the sands from which we vainly attempt to understand the power and fragrance of wind. The ancients knew the vanity of looking into our skulls to become experts of what is within our ribs.

When the Egyptians embalmed a body they first extracted and discarded the brain. The heart was revered as well in the Mayan traditions. It was their highest sacrifice. The heart never demands that we choose it instead of the mind. Hearts always will harmony with all that exists, temporarily or eternally. Our heart wishes only health, wealth, and happiness to all its neighbours, nearest of which are our own minds and bodies.

Modern science is returning from its major walkabout in the shadows of life. The familiar yet mighty universe of the ancient seers, physicians, and scientists is again coming into view. Today's glimpse of science's horizon brings hopeful news of our remembered homeland where mind, body and heart flourish harmoniously. Neuroscientists report that the heart begins to beat in the unborn foetus before the brain has formed. They have also discovered that the heart has its own independent nervous system with over 40,000 neurons.

Feelings and intuitions from the heart have a profound effect on the brain, whereas the influence of the brain's conscious impulses known as thoughts is as negligible to the heart as a single footstep in a mile long stroll. Electromagnetic energy of the heart was measured to be 5,000 times greater than that of the brain, detectable up to three metres from the body with physical instruments. It is no wonder that sensitives and seers gain so much vital information from accessing the heart's powerful life force rather than the outer mind's relatively feeble and short-lived thought waves.

Our brain has two parts to it, the left and the right brain. Each half is responsible for different types of thought available to our mind and body. What we think depends on which side of our brain is dominant at that moment. Also, the side of our brain that is dominant depends on what we will to think. The right side of the brain is imaginative and intuitive, loves painting, dancing, music, healing, and other creative and self-expressive ways of life. The left side of the brain is logical and analytical, developed in school through rote learning and exams designed to test skills in reading, writing and arithmetic.

When our soul receives information from the Spirit world, it is detected in our hearts and transmitted to our brain. Waves of full thoughts and feelings as well as linear nerve impulses are available to the brain's right and left sides, our inner and outer minds. Our right-brained understanding is the result of our heart's translation of Spirit communication into intuitions and visions. Our left-brained characteristics are utilitarian, limited in their applicability by the history of our body and mind experiences.

Our right side of the brain uses our imagination and intuitive sensing to process our heart gifts wholly. This is our inner mind. Our intuition is a form of instinctive knowing not needing the reasoning processes of our left-brain. Intuition is a natural ability of everyone and can be trusted for our guidance, discernment, self-awareness and creativity. We can rely on this wonderful gift every moment.

Information received by the left side of the brain is analyzed, logically or illogically, before processing into mind or body instructions. This is the function of our outer mind. "What happens if I am wrong or if I get a no?" This is your left-brain thinking under the influence of your self, not our heart's instincts. By honouring the gifts and abilities of our whole, complementary brain, we become the communication link between our inner and outer consciousness, walkers between the worlds of our knowing minds and able bodies.

As an example of the complementary nature of our outer and inner awareness, how many of us have been driving along the road when suddenly we realize that we do not remember the bit that we have just driven? What happened was our outer self, mind and body, was in control of driving the car while our inner awareness goes into the dreamtime, day dreaming, disappearing into other worlds. I have spoken to many people about this and they agree that they have been driving for many miles and do not have a recollection of the road that they have just driven. Yet at all times, they knew they were safe.

We experience wholeness and wellness when we integrate our inner and outer sensing and thinking. In the world today, illness is rampant because our minds and bodies are out of balance with each other and with our hearts. We have weakened our connection with a natural way of living. Many indigenous tribes are not diseased and they do not have troubles of the mind or the body. They have stayed connected with their earthly and heavenly homes.

Men especially who have had heart conditions or heart attacks discover almost invariably during their introspective convalescences that they do not know how to love. They have forgotten how to connect with their heart centre. Many times during my readings, spirits who have passed over from a heart attack come to their relatives to say they now understand that they did not know how to love. We can choose before such major traumas manifest to listen patiently to our body with an open and whole mind.

What is it at this moment in time that your body is trying to teach you? Look at your symptoms, which are the effects, and be courageous enough to seek out their primary physical and emotional causes. Feel how any manifestation of incompleteness in yourself is affecting others in your life. Listen to the cries for help from so many people as a guide to what your body or mind may be crying out to you for. I have experienced this process myself many times.

I have suffered much pain through my loss of mother and father, through rape and the loss of my child, and through the break-up of relationships. If you cannot yet avoid causing your illnesses, at least you can change your early symptoms into positive calls for love. Negative feelings of mind or body upset our balanced nature. I find that Spirit thoughts, whether visions or advice, are always life affirming. I trust Spirit completely.

Fifteen years ago I was not well. I underwent surgeries and was still having problems. The doctors I visited said it was just an irritable bowel and gave me tablets for the severe pain. Then Spirit told me to go to New

York straight away. I was used to jetting off to New York City on business every month. It seemed like I just unpacked from my last trip when off I went again. I headed straight to the hotel in Manhattan where I usually stayed, only to find it full up.

The nearest place I located that night was in New Jersey. As I was finally checking into my room I collapsed and was rushed into hospital. I remember hearing the doctors say I was very lucky to be alive. They diagnosed septicaemia and a blocked bowel, but I had come to the right place. This hospital was one of the few that had the special laser equipment needed for my life saving operation.

I spent over three painful weeks in hospital recovering. Then, one morning at dawn, I was alone in my double room when an angel appeared. She explained to me that this ordeal happened because of the contract I had taken out on my self many years ago. I had declared that I did not want children after what had happened to me over the years.

As the angel reminded me, my illnesses began shortly after that decision of mine. I had one operation after another until I had no womb, no ovaries, and just enough of my insides remaining. Here I was living in hospital and now aware that I caused my own cancer. The sudden knowing that my mind and body had listened and responded to my self's wish for no children stunned me. Because I was raped as a teenager, I felt diseased. I wanted to get rid of what was inside me. Well, I did a good job.

Lying in a hospital bed, I began my mature understanding of healing. I thanked the angel who had come to me and she was gone. Just then, a nurse came in to let me know that another patient would be joining me shortly in the room. When they wheeled in my new companion I saw by her attire that she was a nun. She lifted her face to tell me her name was Catherine, and I saw her spirit. She was the angel who visited me an hour ago.

Catharine and I spent the rest of my hospital stay in deep and reverent dialog. She knew she was dying. We would sometimes sit up all night talking about her passing into the Spirit world. Then it was time for me to leave the hospital. I knew that I would not see her again. In a vision I saw her fall out of bed and break her hip, which she did two days later.

Months later when I had fully recovered, I returned to the USA and sought out Catherine's former home, her convent. I visited with the nuns and priest whom I had already met in hospital. I lingered at her gravesite. I will never forget that moment when Catharine's spirit came ahead to visit and comfort me. To this day Catharine is always around me wherever I go. She is my guardian angel. I have had the honour of knowing her in physical form as well, a blessing indeed.

I was the unhealed healer. For some of us it is difficult to accept healing for ourselves. We would rather give all the time. That is not how seers heal. Seers are Spirit messengers of wisdom and love who accept for ourselves the divine truth and beauty revealed to us for others. I am now willing to accept healing for myself from the loving energy that Spirit sends through me for others. I feel and know how very much Spirit loves. I receive with gratitude the many healing prayers sent by my caring friends from all over the world. Angels within and without bless me.

Exercise 3   HEALING OUR SELVES

It is time to know you better. This simple journey of self-discovery takes you to your heart, your wisdom, and your passion.

Find a sacred space in Nature where you will not be disturbed. It can be on the beach, in a forest, in a park, wherever you can lay flat with your arms outstretched and connect with your heart to the Earth. Place a blanket over you if that feels comfortable.

Your intention is your willingness to heal, to become whole and complete again. Your intention creates a circle of protection around you. Lay down on the ground, either faced down or face up, arms outstretched to feel the love of the Great Mother, our lovely planet. Start feeling your own heart beating in time with the Earth. Feel Her pulse.

Listen to everything around you, the birds and animals, the wind, the trees, all of Nature as you allow your feelings and emotions to surface. Just welcome them, become aware of them. When you are ready, merge into the Earth all hurts, all pains, all fears that formed dark clouds over your ever-shining heart centre. Give them to our Mother, and allow Her to take them all away.

Let it go, let the tears flow. Release, and breathe with the Earth until all the unhappiness is no longer there. Now breathe in the healing energies of the Earth. Feel Her love flowing into you, the love of the Great Mother, reassuring you, nurturing you, filling you with love.

When you start to feel a great peace, allow it to flow through you, in and around you, becoming one with your heart. Feel the unconditional love for yourself, for your loved ones, for the whole world. See that light shining out of your heart, reaching and touching life itself.

When you are ready, thank the Great Mother Earth. Know that at any time you can come back to this sacred place to remember your inner healing.

You can spend time each day connecting to your heart. Just place your hands on your heart centre and feel, listen and know. You will be given your answers. It is good to do this in the morning before you start your day's work for it calms you and readies you to be aware of your heart's balance with your head and your heat, your healed mind and your passionate body.

Within the heart is your inner knowing, the real you. Appreciate your heart's wisdom by feeling your soul communicate with your body. Experience your peace of mind as Spirit clears away all old contracts that required your wounds as payment. Void all contracts of suffering on yourself and others because a wise witness never signed them. Get in touch with your heart through prayers of gratitude for the gifts you have already received but were not ready to open until now. Cherish your heart's most precious gift to you, your miraculous life.

CHAPTER 4

TRUSTING OUR SPIRITS

On my fortieth birthday, I got a phone call. "Hello, my name is Jim. I am your brother and I have been trying to find you for thirty years." My adopted mother, my mum, had died four weeks to the day of his phone call. Her last words the evening before she died were, "I do not want you to be alone." She kept her promise. Spirit works in powerful ways. Jim's call opened the door to my entire natural family of seven brothers and our birth mother. It is amazing that my brother has also developed his natural psychic abilities.

I remember being visited by two spirits when I was little girl. They came to me at night saying that they were my grandparents. In these visions my grandfather always had big shire horses with him and I could see a farm in the background. When I asked my mum did not know any of my birth family relatives.

During my first visit with Jim and his beloved wife Catherine after his phone call, I saw on a wall in their house a framed photo of a man standing between big shire horses. Jim had an actual picture of our grandfather, the same as I remember him from my visions. I found out later that my natural grandparents tried to keep me from being adopted. They died without seeing me again. However, they continued to watch over me as loving grandparental spirits, and I truly felt and feel their love.

As children we were all psychic. We were born with this wonderful ability to see the world of Spirit. We naturally loved life and Spirit, delighting in their gifts within and surrounding us. For a moment we were happy souls, believing in fairies, dragons, and invisible friends. They were very real to us. We played, rested, and dreamt with them. They really did exist. Then one day we grew up, and forgot all about our knowing hearts.

Until we see all things again with our inner eyes of love and feel them as alive, we experience the unhappiness of our selves. Our selves harbour all our grievances, worries and traumas. Our heart holds the memory of all our love, given and received. Souls feel our health, happiness and divine evolution. Spirit knows the truth of who we are.

Spirit speaks to us directly from our hearts. This is our knowing feeling called intuition, those inspirations of our inner minds before the outer mind interferes. Souls communicate to our bodies through our hearts as natural feelings, our inner body awareness called instincts. Psychic gifts and abilities are our inner senses.

Like a computer, we do not use all our stored information. We often use what we are familiar with and what we think may work because we do not have time to explore all the information stored in our memory. Our psychic natures are stored in our hearts. We just forgot how to access and use our abilities.

It is the middle of the day here in Egypt and the birds are singing. All of a sudden everything becomes very quiet. I sense something is going to happen. The neighbourhood dogs and house cats disappear. Then the wind begins sweeping the sands in the distance. I feel the dry heat before I feel the force. From our terrace, I see no birds nor hear any animals. People are struggling to maintain their balance as they walk down the street. Cars and motorbikes are weaving with the heaving of the wind.

Just as suddenly I hear the birds again. I know the wind will soon stop and it does so as effortlessly as it started. Life on Earth remains connected at all times of night and day. From amoebas to mammals, natural beings respond knowingly to what is happening in their world. They follow their instincts. They do not think about what they are going to do, they just do it.

Nature transforms life in cycles. Her creations know when it is going to get cold and where to find food. Whales and birds travel thousands of miles to feed and frolic, annually following magnetic energy lines around the Earth. In the modern world we go to the local supermarket for our food following the roads invented for us to drive on. Electric power lines around the Earth connect together the latest electronic devices that attempt to entertain us.

Seers use our heartfelt instincts to work with cycles of Nature and understand how they work. Human instincts use the same instinctive knowing that birds and animals use to guide them away from uncomfortable weather and seasons. Seers also use our intuitive feelings that come from the loving inspirations of our hearts. Inner sensing is an amazing and genuine power that children access naturally. We are all born with natural instincts and faultless intuition but in today's world not all of us use them.

Many of us living in colder climates tend to stay throughout the year. However, more and more people are remembering to follow the sun to warmer weather and away from the winter cold and damp of places like Britain. We are remembering our natural ability to follow the seasons and cycles of Nature.

Our instincts and intuition have been there all the time, they just need to be coaxed out into the open again. We encourage our true feelings and inner awareness and discover a seeming variety of seership abilities. As we develop our psychic awareness, we remember our soul. Our soul knows what to do with our emotional baggage.

Our emotional baggage, our fears and problems, become stuck in us like the clogged drain in a sink. Like me with my ill health, if the emotional pain cannot be released it gets stored as trauma in our bodies and causes more problems. Trauma poisons us and makes us ill. When we work on our personal issues we cannot help but develop our psychic abilities. We receive a lot more information from our hearts because our drain is not blocked.

Seers speak words of truth by opening our minds to the knowing of Spirit flowing from our hearts. The information we receive may be about something we have never thought about before. When this happens our doubting and fearful closed minds try to frustrate us. Our psychic information then becomes clouded over and we will either not give the information we received due to doubt or we will pass it on with distortion during a reading.

Instead of disserving us, our practical outer minds have a natural, more ancient use. Our left-brain thinking is free to listen to our instincts, our gut feelings, and assist our body's wise natural responses to life. We trust these feelings will always be right. Our right brain is free to imagine, to make images of what Spirit gifts to us. It then becomes natural although not normal to hear voices and insistent movements, to see people who are no longer alive out of the corner of our eye and sometimes right in front of us, and to catch sight of bright lights like starbursts appearing out of nowhere.

Many of us remember a psychic experience of one kind or another, and all of us know deep down in our hearts that there is so much more to us than the world encourages. If we trust Spirit we will see, hear, and feel spirits. This experience often takes the forms of tingling throughout the body, a feeling of cobwebs all over our face, tightness in our throat, hot or cold flashes throughout the body, a ringing in our ears, and, of course, goose bumps.

If we go to doctors, they will say there is nothing wrong with us. This is true, spirits are just saying hello. It is your natural body and mind experiencing inspiration, the life and love of our hearts. Seers know and feel extraordinary things about others who we may not even have met before. We connect directly to our inspiration, to the web of life outside of a person's intellect. Our knowing heart sends pictures, symbols and images to our creative inner mind. We pass this information on directly, without interference from our practical outer mind. When we listen to our hearts our open minds offers no judgments, intolerance, or inner critics.

In the modern world we stay busy, thinking and doing. Our minds and bodies seem to forget how to rest and play, to create and to dream. When a natural impulse, an intuition or instinct, comes to us, our minds say, "Hold on a minute, I just have to think about it." I have seen this many times when people are looking to buy something from my shop, and they cannot make up their minds.

They say they will have a think about it and come back later. If they do return, what they wanted is gone. How many times has an opportunity been lost because you did not respond to your psychic knowing, your intuition or instincts? First impressions from within, our knowing feelings, are always right. We avoid problems and save effort when we trust our inner guidance.

Years ago I ran workshops at the local spiritualist church in London. As I was preparing to leave for a workshop one day, my intuition kept reminding me to take the keys with me to open the church door. My mind said, "Don't be stupid. Brian will be there with the keys. He always has the keys." Well I got there and Brian had forgotten his keys. Because I lived nearer, I had to go all the way back to get the keys. That particular workshop I was running was on trusting our intuition. I got the first lesson of the day. We teach what we need to learn ourselves, until we learn.

Inspiration is an awareness not of this world. It connects us to our Heart, the divine Source of all that is natural and heavenly. Seers travel into the worlds of our hearts. We use our inner heart as our primary sense. We see, hear and touch things that are not of this world, yet are real. We remember how to tap into ancient wisdom that comes directly from Spirit and Nature.

When I tap into the Spirit world, I receive inspirations, visions and messages. I live in the midst of a world of spiritual beings, the Elders. I have worked with a council of Elders since I was a child. I have asked for their names and they have always said to me that they have no names and have no need for names. For our happiness they will sometimes present themselves as someone who we will identify with as wise and loving.

They visit here on Earth and live in the heavenly world of Spirit. Decisions that we consider very wise in the ordinary world are very ordinary in the Spirit world. This is because all wisdom and inspiration come from Spirit. Geniuses, bemused artists, and clever dyslexics tap into our spirits and souls for inspiration. We receive extraordinary gifts just for the asking.

Psychic gifts and abilities return with us from all our past lives. In this lifetime we may receive a calling from Spirit or a visit from spirits telling us to develop our abilities as a seer, medium, psychic, or healer. Or we may have made a personal choice after our families grew up to nurture ourselves and develop the psychic gifts that we remember having as a child.

Our psychic gifts awaken in many other ways. We may find our soul through a death and rebirth, a near-death experience, or some unimaginable crisis. You may have had a serious accident, gone into a coma and awakened with profound wisdom. We may visit a sacred sight or meet someone that triggered something deep within us. We might meet a seer, shaman or guru who knows our gifts and abilities and helps us to develop them.

Seers initiate those who come to us for help into the remembrance of who they are. Even though we are born with the gifts, we have initiations. Many of us have experienced the world's disheartening initiations and rites of passage in one way or another. From our childhood we have faced illness, tragedy, loss, betrayal or knowing that we are different. These experiences were either traumatic or we were ready to understand how to integrate this initiation into our life purpose by becoming acutely aware of our surroundings, heightening our sensitivity and trusting our instincts and intuitions.

Inspired initiations give us a deeply satisfying feeling with ourselves. Suddenly we can see out of the darkness that has surrounded us and our life purpose is illuminated. Initiations empower us to feel whole and complete. When initiations are from Nature and Spirit, throughout time this has been the true calling of the seer, shaman, prophet, medicine man and wise woman. We experience the connection to all of life. We are free to live again by our inner sensing and wisdom.

Even the trauma of my infancy adoption did not seem to interfere with having happy memories of resting and playing with Spirit from the day I was born. I have been working with the Spirit world since I was twelve yet I needed the years since then to experience many initiations, rituals and ceremonies on the lands of many countries with people of several cultures and seership traditions.

At 13 years old I was with friends one day playing truant from school. We cycled down to Loch Ness from Inverness. It was a beautiful day so we went swimming and climbed the hills and mountains. We spent the whole day just being in Nature. It was wonderful and freeing. We loved to climb trees, especially one large old oak tree that the four of us tried to climb to the top of.

We were all midway up the tree, when suddenly we heard a loud crash. A big branch from above broke off and narrowly missed us. The tree was hit by lighting. We all felt a tingling, but otherwise we were fine and just laughed it off as teenagers do when we are up to high antics. A few days later, I was washing my hair when my mother passed by and noticed a red line down the back of my neck. This was my gift from the lightning. In that same month I started my first bleed. My initiation from the elements was also my rite of passage into womanhood.

I have had a lifetime of initiations into knowing who I am and releasing who I am not. About five years ago I told friends about my vision of being in the Great Pyramid for four hours on my own in the pitch dark. They asked me how it would be possible. I had been to this sacred site many times and I knew how difficult it was to be on my own inside for such a long time.

I arrived in Cairo and was met by my friend Fergany, who runs trips throughout Egypt. I told Fergany about entering the Great Pyramid on my own for four hours. His reply was that he did not know how this was going to happen unless I paid $1000 to have time on my own. This option was not possible. The next morning we arrived early at the site to buy one of the 150 tickets issued for the day. We were told the pyramid was closed without knowing the reason for this closure.

We went to the entrance where Fergany knew the guards and he spoke with them. A moment later he looked at me and said I had my wish. The pyramid was closed because there was temporarily no electricity. I looked at Fergany expectantly and he said it was time for my initiation.

I did not have a torch to carry. I knew the Great Pyramid well as I had been in it many times. However, going in with no light was a very different experience. I started my way up into the main shaft that leads into the main hall with all sorts of thoughts going through my head. As I entered the Grand Gallery, my heart was pounding.

I went into the Queen's Chamber, banging my head along the way, as the roof is so low. I sat down, trying to still my mind from asking so many questions. Trust me, I faced every fear that I could imagine. I cried, shook and released my fears. When I finally felt at peace I continued on my ascent into the King's Chamber.

As I walked I chanted, and the sounds and energy uplifted me to a heightened state of trance. I was back in ancient Egypt and was taking part in a grand ritual. I could smell the lotus flower perfume along with the smell of sandalwood, myrrh, and frankincense. I heard the sistrums and the chanting of the priests and priestesses. I was a young girl who wore a white dress. My skin was very dark and my hair was in braids. I chanted words that I remember as being old, the names of God and the Goddess, as I ascended into the King's Chamber.

The chamber was charged with energy as I walked in. I could see Spirit orbs flashing throughout. As I continued walking, the energy bounced off the walls and the chants kept repeating. The sound flowed through me. I became the sound and there was no separation. I went over to the sarcophagus and lay down inside it. As I lay there I could feel all the people who had lain inside before, connecting like me to the divine cosmos.

There came a sudden silence. The chanting stopped. I lifted my arms out, reached for the heavens, and called out "I am ready for initiation" three times. In that instant, the electric lights came on.

Even to this day, when I think about my sacred time in the Great

Pyramid I can still feel that amazing energy coursing though me. Of all the sacred sites I have visited, seen and felt, this experience will forever live in my heart. Spirit told me the truth. I did spend four hours in the dark on my own in the Great Pyramid. My vision showed me what was going to happen. I trusted totally, and walked into the initiation with an open heart. I believe in, rely on, and experience miracles.

Seers are aware of the energy within us and around us. We keep our heads in the Sky and our feet on the Earth. We remind ourselves of our divine protection day and night, whether visioning or dreaming. There are many techniques to use for psychic protection. One of the simplest and effective ways is going into our heart centre and visualizing a white light shining forth and surrounding us with pure radiant love. We then strengthen this light with our intention so that our brightness will only attract the same unconditional love.

Our heartfelt intentions create protection. When we trust our heart's wisdom, we experience love around us as a shield of protection. Look at who is around you and why to understand what you need for your psychic protection. While we are still practicing or trying to be spiritual beings, our outer mind's negativities and fears get in the way. When we experience envy or other disempowering emotions directed at us, it can cause problems if we are not feeling protected enough.

Sometimes it is comforting for Spirit workers to wear symbols of protection to remind us of our inner peace. I remember how I used to do a ceremony every day. I put on many necklaces, bracelets, and rings to protect my self. Then one day Spirit told me that my intention was the most important thing to remember about protecting myself. Without the intention of our hearts, ceremonies and rituals will not work. Psychic protection summons forth our soul's powers, our instincts for life. When we trust our souls we feel safe. When we trust Spirit, we know our way.

If we want to drive to a friend's house we get in our car and drive directly there. We first ensure that our car is working, the oil, petrol, water, and tyres are okay, to feel safe and protected. We check the condition of the roads we will be driving, avoiding roadblocks and traffic jams, to arrive at our destination as quickly and as safely as possible. To visit the Spirit world seers also travel directly with no stops in-between. We feel safe and protected, we keep in mind where we are going and how to get there and we arrive at our destination the easiest way possible.

For protection and healing, the ancient Egyptians used amulets in their everyday life, which are empowering symbols with magical words. Today in Egypt when people need protection or healing, they go to the sheik. He empowers them by many means, including an amulet made for wearing next to their heart to ward off unwanted energies. There are many amulets of protection for sale in the shops, including crosses, ankhs, stars of David, and pentacles. If one feels right for you, look into the history of the symbol to understand why it calls to you. Then wear it with confidence and assurance.

Symbols have communicated our relationships with the heart worlds since the beginning of time. Not all symbols of protection are for wearing. Gates are symbols of power and authority. When I walk around the sacred sites here in Egypt, I look for where the gates or doors used to be in the temple structures. At the tombs we can see on the floors and walls where the doors and gates once were. In Abul Simbal the door is massive and so is the key. Places like Karnak were built on a grand scale, with many entrances to the temples and to the inner sanctums.

In ancient and mediaeval cities, gates and doors had their gatekeepers, the guardians who kept out unwanted people and assured those who lived within the walls of their rightful home. They were the protectors of the city and temples and had the great responsibility of being keepers of the keys. The same function of gatekeepers exists in the world of Spirit.

Shamanic cultures, as in West Central Africa, honour the Gatekeepers of Spirits by giving that title to the seers of their tribe who open and close the dimensional gates to the other worlds. In the Wiccan traditions, we call on the guardians and gatekeepers of the directions to protect us when working in ritual.

Seers are able to communicate with any spirit we wish. We go to our guardians, the gatekeepers of the Spirit world, and ask for help and advice. Each of us has a guardian angel, a helper or a Spirit guide. They can be as many or as few as we want. My Spirit guide, Touch the Clouds, has been a very important part of my life. He has been there as my Spirit father, protecting me and loving me just the way I am. He has stood by as I have hurt myself by repeating the same mistakes. Like a loving father, he always nurtures and supports me. He totally understands me without judgment or ever a harsh word.

I always dreamt of going to the USA. I wanted to go where all the native people lived. I was still seeing these lands as if from a past life when we lived in tepees. I flew to Denver and drove to places that magnetized me. It was a magical mystery tour. I trusted where Spirit led me. I will always remember going into my first trading post. I headed straight to a card stand with pictures of native American Indians from the 1880's.

As I turned the stand around to view the other cards, there was Touch the Clouds beaming from the postcard. In this artist's portrait he was standing tall and proud just as I have seen him. I remember him touching the ceiling in my room he was so tall, and here he was. On the back of the card it read, "Touch-the-Clouds, Miniconjou leader, 7ft tall, cousin and friend of Crazy Horse." I just could not stop crying. All the doubts placed into my mind by other people left me. I was free to know without a doubt that he was my gatekeeper, guardian, and Spirit father.

Since then I have had many people confirm my knowing of him. Once I was in Italy and was taken to meet a straga, an Italian witch. When I walked into her room she stood up and greeted me with these words. "There is a tall man standing beside you. He tells me he is your guardian. His name is Touch the Clouds and he is your Spirit father. He is very proud of you." She then sat down and continued for a while to tell me things about my past and self.

Do you remember when you were young being told by the people you shared your Spirit visions with to not be so silly, it is only your imagination? Were there times you have not bothered to discuss your Spirit experiences for fear of rejection? Your imaginary friends were very real. They really did exist. They are your Spirit family, your guides and helpers, and they are still in your heart. They are waiting for you to open up the doors and gates that you have shut but maybe not locked on them for all these years.

In the following exercise, you will use your intuition again while we journey to where your Spirit family is always ready for you. For them it was only an instant ago since you last rested and played together. They are ready to help open up your mind to your heart's knowing, and for you to allow their love to flow through you. It is time to be present in your life once again to the happiness, joy, and wonderment we all once knew when we trusted our spirits.

Exercise 4   TRUSTING OUR SPIRITS

Set aside an evening to work with your gatekeepers and guardians. Just as in ancient times in this world, gatekeepers in the Spirit world hold the great responsibility of sensing who is welcomed. They are your helpful Spirit guides when working with your intuition, psychic abilities, and your seership. They ensure that only the highest energy of love will pass through the gates of the Spirit world to you.

They have a great love for you and have been with you since you came to Earth. They could be people you have been with in other lifetimes who have helped and guided you, or they could be relatives that you knew in this lifetime who have since passed on to the Spirit world. Gatekeepers are always spirits of wise old souls who speak of who you truly are, have been and will be. They are concerned with our highest good, upholding the integrity, truth and honesty of the information we receive from the Spirit world. They ensure it is truthful and precise by remaining our perpetually clear channels.

How we feel and what we believe attracts the same knowing vibrations in the Spirit world to be with us, They are always with us, never opposed. Heaven and Nature are ever harmonious. When we really get to know Spirit, we remember our souls. We feel how kind and gentle spirits are and do not feel like our Spirit journeys are work. They bring us peace of mind.

Veils to the Spirit world are thinnest at dawn and dusk, so arrange your evening journey as near to dusk as possible. If you love to be out in Nature, go to your sacred place outdoors. Otherwise, choose a room where you will not be disturbed. Where are you drawn to be this evening? Trust your intuition and be led to a place of beauty for your first meeting with your gatekeeper/s.

Take a rest from your mobile phone, your family and friends. Create your sacred space with your intention and love. Light candles and make a beautiful and inviting healing space. Sit in a good chair so your back is straight, or if you are in Nature, a good tree can serve as a backrest. Before you sit in Nature, sense how the local souls of the dragonflies, dandelions, creepy crawlies and fairies, welcome you.

Trust everything that comes to mind from within, from your intuition. Use your imagination to help you see clearly. Focus on your breath, becoming aware of your breath flowing through your body. Gently focus your awareness of your breath in your heart centre. Slowly breathe your sacred breath from your heart centre. Feel your sacred heart slowly pulsing in harmony with your sacred breath.

Feel your sacred energy, your soul, expanding outward and inward as your love, light and inner warmth becomes stronger and lighter.

As you expand, open your inner mind to your intuition, your psychic gift from your heart. Feel the expansiveness of you, the real you. Feel as your soul, not just as yourself. Fill your whole being. Feel the warmth radiating from your heart. Expand this feeling until it surrounds you, as far as you wish.

Strengthen your feeling of protection with light of any colour you wish. Feel your soul energy. What does it feel like, what shape is it, how big is it? Stay with this feeling until you know from within that it is time to meet your gatekeeper.

When you are ready, you discover you are now facing the only gate inside the walls of your temple complex. You feel assured by the strength of these massive walls. As you gaze at the gate, slowly become aware of how big it is, what it is made of and how strong it is.

While you are taking a good look at the gate, you notice beside it a gatekeeper's house inside the temple walls. When you are ready, walk over to the door of the house and knock. Feel your sacred breath as you wait for the moment your gatekeeper opens the door.

As you stand there relaxed yet alert, you see that the door is open and the gatekeeper expects you. You instantly remember this gatekeeper. In your absence, your gatekeeper has guarded your inner sanctum, your inner temple inside these massive walls.

Feel the unconditional love of Spirit shining forth from your gatekeeper for you. They are honoured and pleased that you have come to welcome your Spirit family back into your life. You remember and talk about all the times you have had together. When you are ready, you walk with your gatekeeper to your special place.

Your gatekeeper takes out a key and places it into the lock. The door creaks open. It has been such a long time since you were last here. Eons of time may have passed. The room brightens the wider you open the door. You see an altar and a seat in front of you. Your gatekeeper invites you to sit.

You feel at home, as if you have sat in this chair many times. Your gatekeeper picks up a necklace from the altar, the one that has been on the altar since the last time you entered your inner sanctum. It is your necklace, your symbol of protection. Your gatekeeper places it around your neck and speaks to you of a time long ago when you were the seer, the one who knows.

You feel blessed by such honouring. You feel encouraged enough to ask your inner seer to come forward. You allow your inner sight, your seer's eye, to open. Trust your intuitions with what you see with your inner vision. Feel yourself as a seer, awakening the ancient wisdom within you. Go to the very core for the truth, to the inner fire that burns within our Heart. Enjoy your adventure into the realms of your inner knowing, the pathway to Spirit.

While you continue to rest alertly within your inner sanctum, you feel and know deep within your self that you are the inner seer. You are the light of your own heart.

When you are ready, get up from the chair and place the necklace back on the altar. As you do, your gatekeeper tells you it is for your protection. Because you always have the protection of the Spirit world, you can wear it anytime as a reminder.

You walk out of the inner sanctum and your gatekeeper locks the door, telling you that you are welcome back anytime. Your gatekeeper is always ready for you. You will always be safe and well within your sacred space. Nothing and no one can enter in here without your gatekeeper's permission.

As you walk together back to the gate of your pathway to the Spirit world, you express your gratitude in your own way. You know that you will see your gatekeeper again soon. While you stand there having one last long look at your temple of divine love, you effortlessly arrive back to where you have been sitting in Nature or in your room.

In spirit you have brought back your necklace of protection. Do you have one like it you can wear? Can you make it? Could you find it in a local shop?

Give thanks to the sacred space where you have rested. If you are in Nature, thank the caretakers of the land and leave offerings for the animals or elements. If at home, as you put out your candle send healing energy to your loved ones in the Spirit world, thanking them for being with you. When you go to bed tonight you will have a deep and peaceful sleep, knowing you are always safe and protected by the world of spirits.

CHAPTER 5

HEARING OUR SPIRITS

I knew my adopted mother did not have long to live. I asked when she would die and Spirit gave me a date. I knew I had to change things between us, so I wrote a letter to her. In it, I told her that I did not want to continue with all the upset and emotional blackmail. I was 35 years old and my mother could still not say to me the three little words that would make all the difference: I love you.

She did not know how to love herself because she was not loved deeply by her parents, nor were they loved enough by their parents. All she could say in response to my "mum, I love you," was "you, too" It is amazing how three little words from our mothers, fathers and grand-parents would have made all the difference in this world to us. If they let us know beyond all doubt that we were loved by them from the time we were conceived, especially when we were infants, it would change how we view and respond to the world today. Our lives would be so different.

I spoke to Spirit and asked that my mother see the light before she left this world. Then the miracle happened. Mum visited me when I was living in London and the only room I had for her to sleep in was the Spirit room where I did all my readings and healings. She came in for breakfast one morning, looked at me differently and said she had a very strange dream last night. My mother had never acknowledged her dreams. Until that moment, she was a firm atheist and had dismissed my work whenever I tried to talk to her about it.

She explained to me that in her dream she was in a biblical village. A man named Joseph came to her and let her know that he is one of my Spirit guides and would be taking care of her when she passed into the Spirit world. He then explained to her about my work and made clear what it meant to me.

Everything changed between us after her meeting with Joseph in the dreamtime. My mother became a different person. She was now kind and able to say she loved me and how proud of me she was. For the next several years we travelled together to the USA and to Ireland, where she always wanted to visit. In Ireland she discovered a past life. Those years travelling together were the happiest days of her life.

Then came the time when I knew she would pass into the Spirit world. She fell, broke her hip, and went into hospital. By that time she also had terminal cancer. The combination of the two traumas was too much for her body to overcome. Within a week she knew was dying, so I asked the nurses to move her into a private room. That night she went into a coma. I sat with her all night, listening to her laboured breathing and asking Spirit to take her.

Just as I said hello to the Sun as it appeared on the horizon next morning, I looked over to my mother and said goodbye. I saw a light shining around her as her soul left her body and headed straight for the Sun, which now appeared to have an amazing cobweb surrounding it. Mum was on her way Home. Spirit waited until the Sun came up, the time of the day I love the most, so that I would never forget her love for me. The joy we shared during her last years made up for all the times of misunderstanding. She had indeed seen the light.

I asked for a miracle and I received many. Spirit gave me the exact date of her passing so that we could do all the things we wanted to. I never told her I knew the date. I just said, "You never know what's round the corner, so let's go and do it now," and we did. I asked Spirit for her to see the light and she did by seeing Joseph in the dreamtime. The letter I wrote to tell her how I wished to know her love for me was fulfilled.

It is time for us to ask for many things in our psychic, mediumship and seership readings. Spirit has told me ever since I was a little girl to ask and receive and I have always trusted this guidance. Seership is a way of life. It is living 24/7 with Spirit and Nature. The heavenly and natural worlds are always awake. They have a voice, and we can listen to their whispers in the winds of time.

Seership is a life's calling and passion. It is not a game of chance or a get-rich-quick idea. We give one hundred percent when working for Spirit and the person for whom we are giving the reading. We are called upon for advice from many different people, yet to Spirit we always answer. We are accountable because our wisdom can affect whether the person's heart or self is listened to. Our work does not stop when we finish the readings. We also nurture and support that person's soul and soul group, in this world and beyond.

We work with unconditional love for others and ourselves to clear up the unresolved issues from our pasts in this and all other lifetimes. We become an empty vessel when we travel into the heart worlds and see with inner all-knowing vision. When we are authentic, working from our heart centres of love, we enjoy what we are doing and who we are being. We are in integrity. Our minds are open to receive and communicate Spirit's visions through our psychic gifts of clear inner sensing, seeing, and hearing, fancily called clairsentience, clairvoyance, and clairaudience.

The clearer we are in mind and the healthier in body, the steadier we are in our character and the more truthful are our visions. Seers train to remember our heart's wisdom and to differentiate between truth and illusion, reality and nightmares, feeling and fearing, knowing and believing. We are sincere in what we say and do, knowing that this is the only way to be accurate in our seership readings. When we are uncertain about a message from the Spirit world, we are truthful to Spirit and ourselves by asking for clarity. I double-check every communication that makes me feel unpleasant, as I will not give any information that may harm or frighten the person.

We uphold a sacred and ancient profession by speaking the loving truth. We change lives by helping others to change their timelines, to know spirits and remember their souls. Seers discover which of the many different ways to share our hearts' gifts works best for each person and us. The basic difference between a brilliant seer and those who have partially developed their undeniable psychic abilities is that beginners on their path of soul-discovery trust themselves to do Spirit's work. Seers trust spirits will do the work through us. Seers commit to seeing absolute truth through our inner eyes. We are ready to venture beyond our familiar healing tools and mediumship abilities and surrender in total trust to Spirit's certain guidance. This is how we clearly see and understand the visions presented to us.

I travel around the fairs and festivals in Britain and see psychics, healers, and mediums practicing many types of energy work using a variety of tools. I continue to meet many authentic Spirit workers at these shows who do not give their healing techniques fancy or complicated names. They quietly go about their healing in simplistic ways and do not attract attention to their mastery of energy healing. I observe them connecting with the Spirit and natural worlds to effectively balance the energies of their clients.

However, I also notice other Spirit workers looking at their watches, speaking to passers-by during a healing, or attending what is going on around them and not paying full attention during a reading. They have not stepped out of linear time and the habits of the work world. They are limiting their soul power by sticking to their selves in mind or body. Their oversized signs, symbols, and logos are more effective in drawing attention to their selves, not Spirit.

I have heard too many spiritualists speak of love from the platform, who then gossip, criticize and backstab other people because of their own insecurities, fears and jealousies. Spirit does not teach this way. To heal effectively using timelines and soul records, seers know to first clear out our own self-issues. We can then come from a place of honesty to know the past, present and future. We practice what we speak from our hearts, not our selves. Seers talk and walk the way of our all-knowing and ever-compassionate hearts.

Just as philosophy was once a true love of heavenly wisdom and healing was the art and science of mastering the soul's mystery, so is the practice of seership today. Seers integrate our psychic abilities and mediumship skills to facilitate past lives resolution, soul retrieval, shamanic rebirths, inner healing, and other Spirit work. We use our imagination, intuition, instincts, and wisdom. We work through the heart to bring out the poet, writer, singer, storyteller, dancer and musician that live within us. Seers enjoy their work. When we enjoy what we do, we play. Seers play when we work.

Spirit workers are mostly known for prophesies and spiritual insight and for having intuitive powers of seeing, divination or scrying as we call it in my Celtic tradition. Sometimes when we play while working, we use ancient tools of crystal and other stones, cards, stars, water, sand, clouds, fire, and mirrors. We use what feels right to help us see into the past, present and the future. Scrying tools can be the doorway into other times and worlds. Gazing into the object produces a light trance. We receive the information as pictures, symbols, letters, impressions, and sensations.

When I look at the stones, trees, and animals of Nature, I see their spirits. In workshops, I explain to people that when we go back to the very beginning of time there was no internet searching, libraries or books. We connected with the spirits of everything, especially with the first people, the stone people, who are the first ancestors of the land. Now, we can return to these most ancient wisdom keepers and read their records. These records are visible to our hearts and invisible to selves.

If we want to know about a certain stone or a crystal, we take it in hand and sit with it. It does not matter which hand we have it in. What is important is that we connect with the spirits of the land it came from. When we work with different stones and crystals, we often are given information that is different from what is written in books. Spirit information is different for everyone, and what we glean is correct for us. No two stones or crystals are the same because every natural thing has different matter and a unique soul.

Seers know all life as sacred, and we see all motion as life. Many of us visit sacred sites around the world. When we are there, we often collect stones to bring back with us. Interestingly, once back home we may do nothing with them. Stones from sacred sites or anywhere else that we feel a connection with have a record of all time within them. They have the memory of when we were there in our past lives. What we actually do is bring back a record of information. We may have a library of information surrounding us with all our stones that may be just idling on shelves, waiting for us to pick them up and learn.

We can unlock the information relevant to us when we sit with our seer's stone or crystal. Seers use tools, or we go directly to our gatekeepers and Spirit guides when connecting with and assisting Spirit. Regardless how we are given visions, we ensure that the message is delivered correctly to the persons concerned. It is not for us to interfere or change the meaning of the communication. If we ask Spirit directly for information, we will be given the answers exactly as intended and needed at that moment for the good of the person.

Sometimes I find that I am not able to answer questions asked of me by the person I am doing a reading for. Spirit tells me that the person needs to see, feel, or listen to their own answers. I was at a psychic fair in Jersey with a woman who sat with me for a reading. The Spirit world let me know that she had just gone round to every psychic in the hall looking for the answers that she wanted to hear. Of course, she was astonished that Spirit knew. Spirit further said the psychics she had already seen were only given what she needed to know for her own good. Until she was willing to listen to the words intended for her heart she would remain in a place of unrest.

She was ready to understand how her self was clouding her mind from knowing the truth. When we listen to ourselves we only hear what we want to or do not want to hear. Selves seek and ask questions with no intention to find answers. Hearts have answers with no need to seek or question. Nature, souls, angels, children and seers follow Spirit's will without a choice or question. When we listen, see and feel with our hearts, we know without doubt. Psychic gifts flow effortlessly when our selves are out of the way.

Seers give what we get without interference. We do not allow our doubting self-mind to get in the way. Seers remove doubts and fears by working through our hearts. Our souls are who we are on Earth, without a doubt. We are prepared to receive the answers and no longer be deceived by our selves. We deny ourselves the gifts of our soul and the Spirit world when we do not listen to our hearts. Denial is not a river in Egypt. By understanding the difference of what our selves do to us, and what spirits and souls do for us, we are able to help others become aware of their hearts.

Seership is being our own teacher. We consult our inner seers, our spirits, for all answers. Most of us were not taught in our childhood homes, churches, or schools how to access our hearts to receive the answers that we need. Yet everyone with psychic gifts in whatever work we do with the Spirit world can see into our own soul records and those of others. When we access our soul records we see the visions of truth for all time.

The revelation of the secrets of all time depends upon our interpretation of the visions, prophecies and dreams that we are given. In the world of souls we slip in-between time and either speed up or slow down our experience of time. This is how we access the timelines to time travel. Mystics and seers have always known that time travel is possible and that there are other worlds. Seers go on adventures with our souls, always under the trusted guidance of our spirits.

Seers verify repeatedly when working. I ask Spirit for the highest good of the person receiving the message. This is always our souls' only will. I also verify everything so that I am not deluded or deceived. In this work we are conscious of all our own thoughts and emotions. We are able to know when our outer mind is helping or interfering with our clarity when walking between this world and the Spirit and natural worlds. Our own sincerity is the standard for knowing how accurate our seership is.

During readings, we work through our heart centres while simultaneously using our minds and bodies to communicate Spirit visions and soul feelings. We train to remember our heart passageways. Our accurate interpretation of visions depends upon our development of courage. Seers are initiated into the great mysteries of life that are freely available to all of us who are willing and ready to see truly. Like attracts like, so if we are grateful all the time then only the graceful aspects of the Spirit world will be attracted to us. If you are negative, despondent, and confused within your own world, you never leave this world's negative energies. The worlds we can access are the reflection of how we feel. What we know is a reflection of the worlds we access.

During a reading, seers are aware of our feelings and emotions. Seers discern between the peace of the Spirit world, the joy of souls in the natural world and the upset of the world of selves. When the emotions and feelings of other people and other souls become intense, we are aware of whether we are sensing for one or many.

Sometimes we may sit up or wake up feeling very strange. It seems that we do not feel like ourselves. This is when we are noticing other people's energies, or we may be affected by the Earth's energies. When many people are feeling dizzy and sick it is often because of all the things that are happening to the Earth at that moment. We ask Spirit to know whether it is another person, the Earth, or us that does not feel well. Seers are here to respond to calls for love without becoming stewards of negative emotions, whatever their origin.

I prepare for seership readings by showering or having a bath with natural oils, and wearing clean clothes. Then I prepare my reading room with candles and incenses to create a sacred space. Before every reading I step out of the room to cleanse the space. It is like a waiting room in a doctor's surgery. How we work as mediums, psychics and seers is that people and their extended Spirit families of loved ones come to us with their problems and issues that they are ready to have resolved.

The Spirit world comes through as the souls the person has loved throughout all of time and as souls who are aware of emotional links between the person and someone else in the world they are eager to contact. They all come with their feelings. The sacred space becomes emotionally charged. The person having the reading is also coming to us to get rid of their emotional and psychic problems, so a moment's cleansing between readings gives both the seer and the next person a fresh space.

Once I have prepared the room I pray to my ancestors, gatekeeper, guardians and Spirit guides, asking for help and guidance in the work I will undertake. I invite Spirit into my inner sanctum to ensure only loving wisdom is allowed to be passed on through me as their Spirit representative. It is the same feeling as having our family and friends around us. We feel supported. We feel their desire for our peace and contentment. Our Spirit guides only know our complete happiness, our soul's delight. Our joy of working with the Spirit world is reflected in our readings.

I only invite in from the Spirit world those energies of loving vibration. Again, like attracts like. I have never met or experienced a bad spirit in my readings and I have done thousands throughout my life. Yes, I felt energies in my many travels to sacred sites and haunted houses. I have faced everything to the limits of my imagination. My willingness to remain aware of my protection keeps me safe at all times. Unloving energies have no power over us when we know we are surrounded with the invincible power of love. Simple affirmations are helpful, such as "I am strong, I am loved and I love myself," to reassure our outer mind it has nothing to fear. We can chant, pray, or whatever makes us feel upbeat and positive. I love to sing.

I go into the heart worlds effortlessly. I visualise it as if I am in an aeroplane flying over the ocean. As I leave this world I see the waters beneath me. The waves and swirling currents have no stability, just like minds of selves. I am not going into the water because I am ascending as high as possible into that beautiful light which contains all the knowing and feelings that I am working with.

When we travel as psychics and sensitives into the light of the Spirit world, we become stronger as we become lighter. As we see the light, we become one with the light. Seers hover between the worlds of spirits and selves. We open our minds to spirits of truth and light. We surrender our bodies to the care of the natural world, the world of Nature, as we all do when lucidly dreaming and soulfully playing.

I will then call upon the ancestors, Spirit guides and loved ones of the person having the reading. I ask for their assistance and cooperation so that their dear one can gently experience their loving truth, however unexpected it may be. My connection with the Spirit world before the reading ensures a supportive bridge of clarity during the reading. We are all ready now to communicate in a heartfelt way.

I usually find that one relative comes through from the Spirit world to be the main communicator during the reading. Once they have spoken to their loved one, they will in turn bring forward the other relatives and friends who wish to speak. From reading to reading the dynamics change, so time and experience aid our understanding of what is happening. When doing readings and demonstrations, I always ask who is speaking from the Spirit world, what their relationship is to the person I am doing the reading for, their name, how they died, and what dates they can give me for confirmation.

I use a tape recorder as well as pen and paper to speak at the same time as I write the information given me. This ensures I do not miss any vital clues from Spirit. When I ask why in particular a certain spirit wants to make contact with the person having the reading, the departed relative usually has the same purpose. They have realised their mistakes on this Earth when they have passed to the Spirit world. They want to say they are sorry for not understanding their loved ones when they had that opportunity on Earth. We can understand this astonishing fact while we are alive and not need to wait until we pass over. It may never be too late to say I am sorry, but now and here is our perfect place for the embraces, the nurturing, and the healing smiles.

During the reading, invited spirits and their loved ones seek healing for hurt and pains caused by misunderstandings and abuses that were not resolved before they died. Mixed feelings need sorting, especially from those who have died suddenly by murders, suicides, or car accidents. They were not able to say goodbye to love ones. These spirits are drawn to this world, waiting for a chance to speak to someone who will help them clear up an unresolved situation.

I was doing a mediumship demonstration recently when the spirit of a young man came forward wanting to speak to a woman in the audience. He asked her to tell his mother, this woman's friend, that he was murdered and was able to give information for his mother to present to the police. The mother later contacted me, and has since gone back to the authorities with this new information.

Actually, she had always known in the way of mothers, but was not confident enough to state so until her son confirmed the information from the Spirit world. Once everything is resolved, the young man will then be free from ties to this world, and will move on into the world of Spirit to be at peace. His mother knows that her son is with her always, and that justice will be done.

Seers work with messages coming in from the Spirit world during psychic demonstrations in front of sometimes hundreds of people. Imagine how crowded such gatherings become with the Spirit families queuing up with equal urgency for every soul in the room. However, during a reading there is often more to work with than these types of Spirit world messages.

When I first meet the person coming for a reading, I always hug them, heart-to-heart, to let them know I care and to make them feel welcomed into our sacred space. I thank them in advance for their trust. This is very important, as we may be working with their personal records and the soul records of all concerned in the reading, whether alive or seemingly dead. I explain how I will be journeying into their soul records to access the details of who they have been, are now in truth, and yet may become. While our souls evolve over time, they also remain ever happy for all time. Our records contain our souls' happy solutions along with our selves' unhappy problems.

I also gain the person's confidence for our travels into their timelines, as usually occurs during a reading. I will look with my heart's knowing at their present lifetime, while simultaneously seeing their many other lifetimes. How we present ourselves as seers to others is how we introduce them to our work with the Spirit world. Spirit wills that we create a sacred, loving and welcoming space, that we greet all as our friends and family, and that we establish a sincere connection during the reading, such as by sitting beside them without a table separating us, if possible.

Spirits know their loved ones are important, special, and cared for. Our readings are a blessed means for their loved ones to experience these feelings. Reunions with loved ones from the Spirit world can be a very emotional time for most people. They are grateful for hugs and having their hands held as they feel the love of spirits flowing through us into their open hearts. Have a box of tissues handy!

Years ago, I was just finishing a one hour reading for a woman, having successfully given her names, dates and the circumstances surrounding the passing of her relatives, when she decided to speak for the first time since I greeted her. She said that what I said was completely correct, but she already knew all that. What she really came to me for was to know if she would win the lottery and get married again.

Every person coming for a reading will have different agendas and questions to ask of a seer. When their request is to know their purpose in this lifetime, or to resolve trauma that seems to elude their understanding, I tell them which of the many gifts and abilities that seers work with will best help them in the present moment. I take the time to sense their readiness for the real understanding of who they are and are not.

If the person is willing and ready for the amazing experience of realizing that their entire existence is an open book to their soul, I will then track back in the person's past in this lifetime to find unsolved issues that wait healing. All healing is of the past, since our unhealed selves only exist in the past. The person and I may begin chatting about that morning's upset or we may go back to their primal wound in this lifetime, which could have occurred any time after their conception.

The essential healing that loosens if not releases all other trauma is the early and ongoing relationships with our parents. Therefore, I especially look for the disconnections between fathers and daughters, and mothers and sons that affect this lifetime's relationships with other people. This will give another opportunity for departed loved ones to come into our sacred space to clear up misunderstandings. To continue their life hopefully, often the person only needs to hear the departed ones say they are sorry and that they love the person now and for all time to come.

Imagine yourself driving along a motorway, bumping into other vehicles and causing many accidents. You stop and help people who are hurt, and learn how your reckless driving is affecting others. Otherwise, you keep driving down the motorway, oblivious to the carnage you are causing along the way. If you happen to glance in your rear view mirror and see your mess, you just expect other people to clean it up.

This motorway is the timelines of our souls and selves, the record of our loving and unloving actions. Our souls are with us now and for all time to help ourselves clear up the damage of our unloving actions and to share with us the happy memories of our loving actions. Our present and future happiness depends upon looking into the past with our non-judgmental inner vision, our responsible gaze into the rear view mirror. We suffer until we release traumatic memories due to misunderstandings and abuse, given or received, with everyone in this and perhaps many other lifetimes.

Many people tell me that their pasts are not important. They only want to know their future or their fortune. Without resolution of the past, our present and future are fated to be a repetition of the same mistakes until in some lifetime or between lifetimes we are finally willing and ready to stop suffering. The only exercise of our free will is to choose happiness now, the only desire of our hearts and souls. Choosing otherwise is the foolish will of our self.

Once we have cleared up any traumas in this lifetime, we may have time left in our reading to travel back into past lives. Again, I look for any unsolved problems that carry over into the present lifetime. Travelling a person's timelines into the past is not the same as a past-life regression. Past-life regressions depend on a willingness of the person to journey with me as their guide. Traditionally, this shamanic journey is just part of the death of self and rebirth of soul.

My past-life regressions are tasters of what the person may wish to further explore during shamanic healing workshops or ceremonies usually of many days length. Unless they have prepared for a regression, rebirth, or soul retrieval, I reserve these powerful techniques for later meetings with them. In the present reading, I invite them to remain relaxed yet alert, and to feel free to look with me into their past along their timelines.

We both are able to see at the same time what has happened in all their previous lifetimes, but the person's own willingness and readiness is the key to their self-discovery. In their soul records, we can both watch the same TV screen together, sharing the same lucid dream which is the totality of their loving soul memories and the regrets, grievances and traumas of their self.

The seer knows and feels the suffering of the person without experiencing their emotions. We help them to see which past events have bound energies as traumas. While holding the vision of the information from their previous lives, I then track forward into this lifetime to explain the causes from their pasts whose effects make up their self today. Healing of their past and embracing their soul awaits their free-will decision.

We change our pasts by releasing the bound energy of regrets and traumas, transforming it into present happiness. The person's willingness to heal their past by forgiving themselves and other selves shifts their timelines to reflect a joyous soul destiny instead of their self's imperfect fate. This process may take many repetitions before the person realizes that they postpone their healing and continue to suffer because of their self-resistance. Until then, the tapes and written records I make for them as we journey become their lessons to learn.

If time permits, we continue to integrate their soul for all time by tracking forward to the future possibilities of their destiny lines of happiness. I know without doubt that we change our fate into our destiny when we finally remember our purpose for this lifetime. I do not tell the person their fortune. I assist people in seeing the likely possibilities open to them. It is effortless for a seer to trace time for information on past events because the past has happened and only awaits our selves to be finished with its lessons. Our soul's beautiful memories for all time return as renewed life when we forgive our selves and others.

It is not so easy to predict the future. Up until the very moment of a future fated event, we can change our minds to listen to our hearts instead of ourselves. We can release our bodies from our self-control to return to our heart's care, and heal. Seers glimpse what will happen based on the fated course of the person's actions in this world. We also gaze into the eternal vision of our resting ancestors: Heaven on Earth.

Seers make no effort to predict what happens in the future, or to speak of what is inevitable based on the destructive practices of selves. This is because we do not judge our Heart's desire for our brilliant destiny and evolution on Earth. Nor do we fear the faded glory of fated selves. What dream we personally and collectively wish to live out on this Earth only time will tell. At the very least, seers give more clarity to a person concerning events before they happen. At the end of the reading, we hand over to them the responsibility for choosing their own destiny.

The more developed we become in our seership skills, the easier it is for us to see into the worlds of Spirit and Nature that are invisible to the outer mind and to simultaneously travel the complete timelines of the past through the present into the future. To see the visions of the truth and beauty of the universe, seers have no choice but to be conscious of who we are and what our purpose in life is. We are vigilant for the destiny our souls wish and spirits will us to see.

To develop our clairvoyance, mediumship, and psychic abilities, we honour our insights into our one reality. We respect our heart's understanding of the worlds of selves, souls and spirits, and are able to distinguish them from each other. We will our minds to remain open to our knowing when weaving between the worlds. We do so in perfect safety. What we see is reality, so there is no problem or danger whatsoever in experiencing self-deception. We go into the heart worlds, gaze into the regions where we find the direct truth and then bring back the pictures within these worlds as we happen to see them through our own imaginations.

I will not bring back any negative thoughts or feelings. I have always had this connection with the Spirit world. Every person that comes to me for an answer or information will only receive the loving truth. This is why during my readings there will be times when someone asks for something and I will not be able to give an answer. What I do then is find something else that they will benefit from knowing at that moment in time. I will be given many signs. At other times, however, I find that I am given information but am just not allowed to reveal it all. Spirit lets me know when there are certain events in the person's future that I can only share when they are ready to hear without fear.

I once had a vision of Swain falling off his farm tractor and injuring his head, which, of course, happened. However, I always had the knowing that I was not to tell him of the vision. Later he confirmed that he also knew it was fated to happen, but he did not act upon the vision. I was much relieved when Swain's seership noticeably improved because of his head injury. It was a powerful lesson for both of us about listening with integrity, and trusting the ways of Spirit.

Years ago when my former husband and forever friend Shaun and I were growing our business together, we had an agent selling our products named Ena. I started having dreams and visions about a motorway accident involving her. I saw the car, the bridge and the out-of-control lorry hitting her car. I ignored these visions as best I could, until one day when I was in the dentist's chair. As I was gazing at the ceiling, the words ENA DEAD clearly appeared.

I went back to the office wondering how I could tell Ena without frightening her. The phone rang and it was Ena. I started speaking with her casually and a moment later a man's voice came from my lips telling her what would happen. Because she now knew about it, she could change her fate to a safe destiny.

Six months went by without anything happening, and both of us nearly forgot about the warning. Then one day while Ena was driving across a bridge on the dual carriageway going into Wales, she had an instant flash back to the vision. In the next moment a lorry travelling in the opposite direction lost control, crashed through the barriers and leapt onto Ena's side of the motorway. Because of her flash warning, she knew what was going to happen and swerved her car out of the way. Both she and the lorry driver lived, thanks to the vision of fate that she changed into her destiny through trust.

Many if not all mediums, psychics, clairvoyants, shamans, mystics and seers go through much trauma and upset during our Earth walks. We do so to learn from our own experiences what we have come again to teach and share. I even find that when I am doing a reading for a person, there will be information for me to absorb as well as for them. Seers have experienced this phenomenon throughout time, and today some call it sound advice.

Our work for Spirit is neither selfish, meaning just to benefit our selves, nor is it selfless, since even the most advanced seers, shamans and gurus must maintain a glimmer of self to remain visible in this world. We know to apply the teachings we receive for others to ourselves as well until we are finished with our own healing. This is every human soul's sole purpose. Spirit does not will healers to remain unhealed. Whenever we give a seership demonstration or receive a healing for someone, we have another opportunity to accept the sound advice or healing for ourselves. By our acceptance, seers no longer teach what we need to learn and preach what we do not practice.

Seers, psychics and mediums receive our Spirit gifts and embrace our soul abilities to benefit all. We move ever lighter in the world with each mystical moment, flash of inspiration and revelation of our Heart's desire. We clear away doubts and fears that have held us back, kept us in the dark and diverted us from our destinies. We become ever more responsible and effective when people come to listen to our wise and compassionate words. Our words have the power to change their worries into happiness. We help people change their lives and to see themselves in the miraculous light of love.

After mum passed, I left the hospital and got into my car. Spirit told me to turn the radio on. As I did a modern cover of Sting's magnificent song started to play, with the refrain "every breath you take, every step you make, I'll be watching you." I knew it was an endearing message from my mother. I went home to her house and slept in her bed. She came to me in the dreamtime to tell me she was okay. The most amazing energy started flowing through me. I felt my mother loving me, holding me, telling me of her eternal love for me. I was in Heaven. So is she.

Two months later I was running a workshop on mediumship development. A participant came to me one day and said he had a message for me that I might think was strange. All he knew to tell me was the name Joseph. He asked if I could understand this, and I smiled gratefully and told him yes. One word from the Spirit world is sometimes all we could possibly wish for. With this gift from Spirit, I knew my mother was safely with my Spirit guide Joseph, as he had promised her.

Shortly after this confirmation, my dear friend Lynn, a sister seer and an amazing psychic artist, presented me with a poem that she had framed and lovingly hand scripted. She made it so beautiful for me to read and reread because a few days before she had received these words in her dreamtime from my mum:

Spirit wants to send a message, a message through a friend
The total reassurance that life will never end
A message in a flower, sent to you with love
And furled inside the petals, a message from above

Always know I'm with you, and try not to be sad
I'm in all that is around you, in the love that we both had
You know when I am near you, although you cannot see
You feel and sense my presence; you know that it is me

I'm part of what you're feeling, the life you've still to live
I'm proud to be your mother; I know how much you give
I'm always here beside you in all you do and say
I'm in the way you think and speak; I guide you through each day

The message we are sending is one that you know well
It's the one you give to others, the one you were sent to tell
Believe what you are feeling, and know that you are right
You choose to live this lifetime; you choose to fight this fight

So think about this flower, with petals soft and curled
Teach it first to open, its beauty then unfurled
And once its hidden beauty is open to the eye
There's no more need for sadness, no more need to cry

Nothing ever changes, know always where I am
As always right beside you, and proud to be your MUM

Exercise 5   HEARING OUR SPIRITS

Working with the Spirit world is as easy as making a long distance phone call. If I want to phone my friend in Australia, I call her direct and if I cannot get through then I speak to one of the operators to assist me with the connection. If you want to speak to spirits then go directly to them. If you are having difficulties getting through then call on your Spirit operator, your gatekeeper or Spirit guide, for their ever-reliable personal assistance.

Once I have established the connection to the Spirit world during a reading, a relative or friend in the Spirit world of the person having the reading comes forward as spokesperson for all the other loved ones waiting to speak to the person. As I am rapidly communicating all the love from the Spirit world, the person often asks me to communicate back to them how much they miss their relatives as well. I tell him or her to speak to them directly, since the connection is already made, the phone line is open, and their Spirit guide is standing by as the operator.

For your call to the Spirit world, take the evening off and go to your sacred space. It is going to be a long distance call, so make sure you are comfortable and that you will not be disturbed.

To make your phone call, you will need a spirit phone, a communication tool. On your altar, you already have a special stone or crystal, or a picture, ring, necklace or other reminder of the loved one you are willing and ready to hear from.

Use whatever technique you have discovered works best for you to enter into the relaxed yet alert state that summons forth your gatekeeper, Spirit guide, or inner seer. They will be your long distance operator for the evening.

Make the connection to your Spirit operator, and ask them to connect you directly to your loved one. Clearly give your operator the name and any special clue to their identity that only you and they recognize. This serves as your secure password. You protect your privacy by trusting that it is impossible for anyone else in the worlds to guess, fake, or assume the significance of your password.

While waiting for your call to be connected visualize your loved one as if they are in the sacred space with you now. Spirit phones are not just picture phones. They have state-of-the-art holographic displays. You hear the phone being picked up at the other end. You did not have to wait long since spirits are never busy, engaged, or disconnected.

You are so excited that you just start talking. You tell them how you are, what you have been doing and how much you miss and love them. Once you finish saying what you have been dying to say, you are ready to listen to them tell you what you have been living to hear.

At first, you may detect only a faint reply from the other end of the line. Ask your Spirit operator to check the connection and have them turn up the volume for you. After all, it is a long distance to the next world until you realize that spirits are as near to you as your sacred breath.

You will hear them clearly speaking with you in the manner that you recognize to be only theirs. They tell you how they are, what they are up to, where they are, other relations they have met, and how much they miss and love you. You wish you had picked up the phone much sooner to hear such good news.

Now they are telling you that there are other relatives and friends waiting to speak with you. You need not worry about the bill. The call is free and you can talk all night if you wish. You never impose on their timelessness. Let every departed soul you recognize on the other end of the line say hello and tell you their stories. Feel their love.

They are explaining to you how they talk to you in the dreamtime and how they visit you every day to make sure you are okay. They tell you about all the strange things that have been happening in your house, like doors opening and closing, objects moving, light bulbs blowing, phones randomly ringing, and electric equipment going funny.

Now you know why you have been turning around when you sense someone is there, or why you see something out of the corner of your eye, smell nostalgic scents, and feel cobwebs over your face. You are relieved to know that you have been feeling them all along trying to get in touch with you.

Now, when you get the funny feelings, all you need to do is pick up the phone, speak direct, and listen. You can call them day or night. They have all the time in this world for you.

Once you have finished your conversation, thank them for explaining everything. You are happy, content, and feel sleepy. They say that is okay, they will see you in the dreamtime. They are always connected to you. You tell them you love them and you will speak to them soon. They wish you happy dreams.

The Spirit operator comes back on the phone and asks if everything went well. You tell them of your happiness and thank them for connecting you to your loved ones. They thank you for your willingness to hear your Spirit family. They remind you that they are available 24/7 to help you connect your heart to all souls on Earth and in Heaven. The lines from the Spirit world to you are always open.

CHAPTER 6

FINDING OUR SOULS

It was dark. There was no one around. I made sure of that. I had planned it down to the last detail. Nobody would find me. This was the right place, the right time. I had taken a concoction of drugs and drink that would kill ten people. I had tried it twice before, taking a whole bottle of valium, and still it did not work. This time it would.

I was starting to feel tired, sleepy, drifting, seeing and feeling a brand new world. The cold of the water no longer affected me. I knew that the concoction would numb my feelings and take away all the external thoughts. My whole life flashed in front of me. So, they are right. I had heard many people talk about this. Just as they were about to pass into the Spirit world they saw their entire lives. Well, I did not want to see mine.

Of the 17 years I had lived on Earth, in this moment I could only remember all the terror, pain, and guilt of the rapes and loss of an innocent child that I had to endure since leaving my loveless home two years ago. It felt like my whole life was shown to me as a living hell. Nobody understood me or wanted to, from my parents, the schools, church, even friends. Not one human had bothered to take the time except Swain, but I stopped seeing him because I was too ashamed to believe any more in what he saw in me.

It was too late now. My hands were getting cold. It was the middle of winter. I was grasping the edge of the bank, up to my neck in water. I was right beside the slush gate in the Caledonian Canal and I could feel the power of the currents dragging me down. It was time to let go, to sink into that loving embrace of my real family. I wanted out of this world, into the next. I knew that there my Spirit family would be waiting for me, the only love I had ever known since the day I was born. Spirit always took care of me, looked after me, and showed me things that I did not think were possible through animals, birds, trees, and the elements of Nature.

Nobody here will miss me. I was always told I was no good, that I was a wicked person, a witch, evil, a devil's child, and strange. What was the point in hanging around? Let me get it over and done with, and then at least I will not be a problem to anyone anymore.

I let go of the bank, and as I did so, the next thing I knew I was being pulled out of the canal by my hair, being dragged up the side and onto the top of the bank. I tried to fight but I was so tired I could not. I thought, "Who is this person? What right have they to interfere with what I was doing? How could they be here?" I was a mile away from the nearest house. It was past midnight and black as pitch, so how did anyone know I was here? They did.

The shock of the night air brought me back to my senses. I was lying face down on the path beside the bank. All I could see was a man's pair of feet in what looked like sandals. I gathered my wits about me to shout abuse at this man who had robbed me of my free will. "How dare you decide for me? I want to die. I do not want to be here anymore!"

The words that came back were to change my life forever. "You have so much work to do, here on this Earth. It is not time for you to die. I know that you will not understand what it is that we have planned for you. Know that your life will be different from now on and that in time you will come to understand who you are and why you are here. You need to trust and remember that everything that has happened to you is for a purpose and in time all will be explained fully."

In my mind I asked, "Who are you?" The answer that came back was, "I am your Spirit father. I am Touch the Clouds. When it is time, you will come back to the land you once knew as Turtle Island, now called America. Remember you are Nature's child, and all will be revealed to you." With that he disappeared. One moment he was there, the next one he was gone. I was left alone, cold and damp, frozen to the bones. However, inside me I could feel a flame igniting something so deep, so passionate that it would change my life completely, beyond compare.

This was the first of three deaths and rebirths I have experienced in this lifetime. Each one has brought me to a deeper understanding of who I am by releasing me from who I am not. You have probably heard of the expression "I've been to hell and back". Well, that is just what happened to me when I ended up in hospital early in December 2005, fifteen years since my second death and rebirth when hospitalized with dear Catherine.

For two years, I had been in poor health. During this traumatic time of facing my inner child victim issues with James, I had suffered a stroke. My body became toxic from peritonitis and from the large doses of antibiotics that I was taking for it. I experimented with many traditional remedies that might help counteract the draining of my life force. Yet I was still so ill that when I was driving down to the recording studios of Joyaa and Gavin in Devon to cut my latest CD, I begged Spirit to take this disease away from me. Two hours later I collapsed and was rushed into hospital. My appendix was inflamed and the doctors decided to remove it. However, my raging fever postponed the surgery for three days.

When I finally had the operation, it was my first one after 15 years of being clear of the surgeon's knife. Two weeks later, I was still in hospital, seriously ill and running a high fever again. On 21st December the fever became unbearable. I remember wailing uncontrollably. The doctors and nurses said there was nothing more they could do for my fever but wait for it to break overnight.

I was sharing the hospital room during this day with two practicing pagans who were wonderfully compassionate despite their own agonies. Along with James, they kept a vigil for me throughout the long Winter Solstice night as I slipped through the veil of death and returned for the third time in this body. In this near-death experience, instead of going into the light as I had done the previous time with the help of Catherine's angel, I went to hell.

I experienced being in a very dark place feeling stripped down to the bone, no more than a skeleton. I knew that I needed to rebuild myself up from my very marrow. It was a terrifying process. I discovered this hell was the one I had created as a victim of other people's judgmental thoughts and punishing actions during this and previous lifetimes. Toward dawn, I began feeling amazed by how much needless suffering I had endured in mind and body. I shouted from the depths of my being "Enough!"

I knew I could not and would not bear these deadly burdens any more. I made a commitment to my body not to part with any more of its precious wholeness. I felt my soul encouraging me to stop proving myself worthy of respect. I awoke with a deep awareness of innocence washing over the dreadful memories of this lifetime's abuses. For hopefully the last time, I died to who I was not, and was reborn to my new yet ancient soul.

Why did death and rebirth happen to me three times? Because I was severely wounded as a child, I was not understood and my needs were not met. My pain was repressed in my mind and lay dormant in my body waiting to manifest as an illness. My emotional wounds placed great stress on my immune system, which kept breaking down as an adult. The strength of my soul and the gentleness of my Spirit family carried me onwards. I continued to forgive others no matter what, because I knew the love of Spirit and felt the love of Nature.

I understood the people around me were unloving, but my knowing needed to return me to loving myself. My soul, the life and joy of my natural body, became my vision quest. When our minds and bodies are closed to our hearts because of abuses and traumas we lose the instinct to feel, to love, and to have hope. When our passion is lost, our life purpose disappears. This is why when I ask people how I can help at the beginning of a seership reading, many say they are lost souls because they do not know or feel who they are.

Soul loss is actually our loss of soul consciousness, seer's vision and heart wisdom. This loss of sensitivity occurs from our experience of trauma as children as well as when we are adults, in this lifetime or previous ones. We suffer trauma or loss when unprepared for loved ones passing into the Spirit world, break-ups of valued relationships, hateful physical violations, drastic diseases of our dear bodies, and repeated shattering of our child mind's natural innocence and trust.

Seers understand there is no real death, no soul loss, only the evolution of what we do not need for our healthy bodies and whole minds. What we do not need is the unhappiness of emotional and psychic trauma. The transformation from death of the unhappy self to rebirth of our life force, from the release of our treasured heart to its expression as a healthy body and whole mind, is inner healing, alchemy and finding our souls. We release trauma by transforming our fears, pains, hurt and deaths into renewed lives.

What we do is cease projecting the responsibility for our feeling of our soul's loss or death onto someone else. Instead, we courageously face our fears and judgments, no matter their origin, and die to the self who we are not. When we do this we experience the retrieval of our soul and realize our soul never abandoned us. We nearly and merely forgot who we always are. Our souls come to retrieve us.

Shamanic and other seership traditions gift us with ancient under-standings about dying to who we are not and being reborn as who we are. During death and rebirth we receive powerful information and impulses from the Spirit and natural worlds. We do not experience this walk between the worlds alone. Departed loved ones and the ancestors, called by some the ascended masters or Elders, are in the Spirit world to help explain everything that has happened to us. We understand these higher beings by minding our hearts.

When we temporarily pass into the Spirit world we are in the veil, that twilight similar to dawn and dusk. As walkers between the veils we have glimpses of Earth as it is in Heaven. These are our soul experiences of natural and joyous living. The veils are only appearances of separation to our thinking minds and sensing bodies. In reality, our Earth is not separate from Heaven.

To help us understand and prepare for death of the self, seers from many traditions have simplified our understanding of the worlds by explaining them as three: upper, middle and lower. These worlds are experienced by us as rest, work, and play. In the upper world of spirits, we rest peacefully in eternal communion with all souls. We experience spirits in Heaven as Spirit experience us on Earth.

Simultaneously, in the lower world of Nature, souls happily play through all bodies. We experience souls everywhere in our natural universe. In Heaven and in Nature we feel divinely happy because we experience the real protection and nurturing of our Mother and the Father, our God and the Goddess, in their truly beautiful singularity as the One. We create spiritedly and re-create soulfully in our Heart and Home.

When, for even an instant we do not feel happy, we know we have somehow entered into the middle world of our outer minds and bodies, the world of unease, stress, and fear. We experience effort and limits in the middle world and we immediately busy our minds and bodies inventing thoughts and things to reflect and project our suddenly found selves. Until we remember the souls we are by dancing in and out of the veils of the upper and lower worlds with ease, we stay in the middle world of work, the unnatural world of separated selves who forgot our souls' purpose.

We come into our present lifetime from the upper world of spirits and the lower world of souls as divinely human beings. We experience unhappiness because of this lifetime's traumatic events. Unhappy experiences bring about the birth of selves. Selves spend lifetimes wasting our souls' energy on retaining and acting out unhappy memories of their unknowing minds and unfeeling bodies. The modern working world is the invented history of unhappy selves. This is not our happy Earth as Heaven wills and Nature wishes Her to be always.

We suffer from missing expressions of our minds and bodies when we lose touch with our souls' gifts and joyous emotions, when we are not resting in the truth and playing in the beauty, and when our selves have separated from our souls. Soul retrieval seems to be finding the lost parts of our soul, but remember that our hearts and souls are always whole and complete.

Thus, we actually return to our sense of wholeness and wellness by remembering the heart beings, the souls and spirits, the lovers and seers, who we are. We are never alone when we are willing to know our hearts again. Our ancestors, guides, and loved ones from the Spirit world share our reunion celebration with our souls. Seers travel between worlds and along timelines to help ourselves and others who are willing and ready to feel again our eternal souls temporarily residing within our human hearts.

When we do not feel our souls, we have no choice but to project our beliefs about the present into the past and future. To our selves, who we are not, this very moment does not exist. In fact, the first experience we had in this lifetime of who we are not was our first false belief, our first false moment, and our primal trauma. We touched hell, the unreal, the middle world.

When we listen to Spirit we have no choice but to welcome the reality of the present moment. This is the realm of our intuition and psychic gifts, our link with the upper world. When our body naturally listens to our heart's knowing we experience the realm of our instincts, our link with the lower world of Nature. Our spirits and souls see on Earth as above and below and see the present as the focus of pasts and futures.

Seers know that Spirit has no separate mind or separate body, so formless and limitless divinity exists always and in all ways. Our soul is our embodied expression of Spirit and our natural bodies are temporary forms of our souls. All is perfect as created, and evolving as Spirit sees it. Only selves defend their unnatural and unfortunate middle world by calling Nature and Heaven otherworldly.

Ancient seers and modern scientists agree that Nature and Spirit, manifested and unmanifest divinity, are our One reality. Effort, exceptions and personalities have no purpose. By ignoring this wisdom it has become possible in our middle world to experience the seemingly endless variations of unnatural effort called work. Seers help and heal by remembering our naturalness and wholeness. We overlook our own false and unnatural perceptions in all worlds and use our inner senses and inner knowing to remain vigilant for the presence of spirits and souls on Earth.

True messages are loving messages. Seers know that our hearts hold our gifts of wisdom and health. We see into all worlds with relaxed alertness, with the restful and playful nature of our souls. Because we know Spirit always protects and nurtures us, we overlook or brush aside messages that do not resonate with our open loving hearts. Whether doing a seership reading, looking at our own dreams, or allowing Nature to show us Her ways, we know to accept as true what we feel to be loving, our intuitions. We open our minds ever wider to allow our body to respond to what it knows to be life supporting and effortless action, our instincts. Seers are happy souls.

In no worlds or realities is falseness and fear a reflection of our Great and Holy Spirit's nature. I have had no fears of the worlds I have travelled in since I was a little girl. Similarly, I had no fear journeying with sacred plant medicine teachers. Even in the hell of my final rebirthing, I still knew it was Spirit's way of healing me.

Our outer minds are our selves' made-up inner world. Without self-serving minds, our bodies may be harmed, but we will instinctually continue to survive, evolve and transform according to Nature's impartial, holistic wisdom. Instincts direct our natural child bodies to seek without and within for warmth and nourishment, to confidently and courageously survive and to sense and feel life.

Selves think without Spirit. The inhuman, heartless, merciless, unfeeling, soulless, and utilitarian middle world is invented by thinking without Spirit. This unnatural world is not real because it is not like the wise and loving worlds our hearts see. Thus, our selves are at home nowhere in reality. Because selves are separated from wisdom and love, they think in terms of avoiding or facilitating destruction and death and react accordingly.

Selves take a holiday from their nowhere homes in their made-up minds and invent a world on Earth and now even in the heavens. In the world, selves experience effort instead of ease, work instead of play, and sickness instead of health. Selves are in neither Heaven nor Nature, and if it were not for our souls and spirits, this middle world would be all there is on Earth.

Selves think of many ways to avoid looking inward and outwards upon our divinity, our hearts treasures of truth and beauty, our spirits and souls. Yet we inwardly sense that there is life after physical death, as well as before we are born. Our hearts and souls do not feel or know death because it is not a thing or thought of Spirit.

Seers experience what the Australian Aboriginals call the dreamtime; that life in this middle world is but a dream to our souls. I have seen the world's dream nature, and I understand its symbolism. When we experience death of self before physically dying, we see images that cannot harm us because they are as dreams. We need never be afraid of these images, no matter how sensitive we are.

Evil worlds do not exist to souls so they are unreal to the seer. The seer's worlds are not frightening plays starring corpses and devils. Seers live as our spirits will and our souls wish. Our hearts guide our natural bodies and open minds to serve Spirit and Nature passionately. Reality to the seer is our heart's experience of intuitive wisdom and instinctive feeling. Bodies and minds are purposeless without our heart's love. A body without feelings and a mind without wisdom are lost in all worlds.

We can integrate our mind and body with our heart while still alive on Earth and experience this middle world, this lifetime, as Spirit wills. Spirit does not know of punishment or penance, so the rules of the schools and churches of our fearful world are not as Spirit wills. Spirits and souls gift only miraculous abilities. Seers bring Spirit visions of health, wholeness, and holiness into this world. We bear compassionate witness in this world to all innocent souls not listened to by suffering minds and bodies.

Seers remember our naturalness expressed through playful bodies and innocent minds sensitive to the souls of all things. We heal by opening the outer mind to our heart worlds and gift from our inner knowing to the outer world. When our minds are consistent with our wise and caring hearts, our bodies naturally reconnect with our life force, our instincts, and our passions. Thus, we open our inner eye to see this middle world as viewed from the heart worlds and are free to travel fearlessly between the worlds as messengers of hope and grace. We do not wait until the death of our physical bodies to sense the rapture of Spirit.

My three journeys into the Spirit world during the instants of my physical death were my rites of passage through all the worlds of Spirit, soul and self. I have experienced transformation to a new me, who I am, from the old me who I was not. They were my initiations from all that was unreal, the middle world of my self, into the worlds of my heart. For the first time in my life I am living between all the worlds in bliss. As a seer, I journey in the upper world of the angels and gatekeepers for guidance and creativity, in the middle world for healing my self and helping others heal themselves, and in the lower world for shamanic and playful reconnection to all souls.

We have no fear of things when we accept them as no longer worthy of frightening us. I have experienced the cycle of birth and death and rebirth, so I know there is no death of who I am. I commented at a workshop only a few months ago how I felt so much better since I died. I have ascended the tree of life, the tree of knowledge and bliss, through all my experiences. I am reborn and blessed indeed.

The tree of life is a very important symbol for nearly every culture. The ancient Celts believed that all trees were wise and old, and that trees bridged the gap between the upper, middle, and lower worlds. Trees were sacred when the Druids walked upon the ancient lands of Britain. Trees were the ancestors of the land, connecting our impulsive souls with the world of patient spirits.

Trees symbolized the entire cosmos connected as One. The oak tree is the centre of the universe, the passageway into the other worlds. The Celtic word for oak is daur, the origin of the word door. Oak trees are doorways to the other worlds, guarded by the doorkeepers.

Since I was a little girl, I have played in trees, slept under trees, talked to trees and trees talked to me. As in the movie of the book *Lord of the Rings*, it was very real to me when the trees came alive. I had seen trees come alive so many times, but I had always been on my own until one day when I was able to share this experience with Shaun.

It was New Year's Eve and we were driving through the Four Corners area of the Southwest USA. Shaun was used to the wonderful experiences we had on our travels in the USA. We decided to stay the night at the canyon lodging. The full moon was out so we went for a walk. It was a clear night with no wind. As we walked along an avenue lined with trees, one tree started to shake and rustle. All the rest kept perfectly still. We went over to the tree and Shaun said he would not have believed it unless he had seen it. I turned to him and said I have believed it all my life, which is why I see it.

Miracles happen every instant. When we believe in them, we see the worlds of spirits and souls in harmony. We see their true unity. Human beings have stood in between the two worlds and divided them. Seers are the bridges, doors and trees, joining all worlds into one reality, one life and one Earth.

Exercise 6   FINDING OUR SOULS

It is time now for you to be with Nature and your soul. When it is possible, spend a day being with trees, the standing ones. Find a sacred grove, the dwelling place of goddesses and gods, or a place in a park, or trees near a river or lake, or near a beach, wherever feels right for you. All of us will have different trees that we love depending on where we live.

Take your time to get to know the tree throughout the seasons, for they are in tune with the cycles of Nature. Get to know the animals and birds that play and live in its branches, roots or trunk. You will find your tree is full of life, waiting to share with you all its secrets. It is here to re-establish a connection with you. Let trees talk to you about how they provided fruit, bark, leaves, flowers, and sap to make herbal and aromatherapy remedies and incenses. They are our Earth's lungs. They breathe for us, and provide heat for fires, wood to build homes, and paper to write on.

It is now time to give back. Go to your favourite tree and ask permission to be there from all the souls and spirits who live at this tree. Make yourself comfortable, with your back against the tree. Make sure you have your circle of loving protection around you so that nobody will disturb you while you are here.

When you are ready, slow your breathing until you can find the pulse of the tree. Now, breathe with the tree. Feel the tree breathing for you. Allow yourself to let go, totally relax, and be at one with the tree.

As you become one with the tree, become aware of your legs and feet connecting with the roots of the tree. Feel yourself becoming rooted with the tree, going deep down into the Earth. Just allow yourself to let go, to sink deeper and deeper down into the ground, to connect with all of Nature, the womb of our Mother Earth. You feel safe and secure. Allow the life energies of the Earth to flow through you. Become aware of how you are feeling. It is a familiar feeling. You are feeling your soul.

Just let go and sink down to the very core of the Earth. Feel with your soul as you visit with the lower worlds. You may have fairies or elves visit you. You may have an animal or many other wonderful creatures come to say hello. Just allow your soul to play.

When you are ready slowly make your way back to surface of the Earth where you are sitting, thanking those along the way who came to visit you.

Now be aware of your presence in this moment. You know your body can sense the middle world we live in at any time, but for this moment stay with your inner sensing. Be with your soul. You may experience a slight misty sensation because for this moment you are between the lower and middle worlds. You are in the veil, a walker between the worlds of souls and selves.

Stay with this feeling as you experience this moment. Reach out and feel the trunk of the tree. If you wish, stand up and hug the tree. Or else, just straighten your back against the tree as you sit. Feel your tree's strength. Feel it supporting you.

Now place your awareness into your spine, whether you are standing or sitting, and connect to the tree so you and the tree are one. Just breathe into the tree. Feel secure, let go of any tensions, fears and pains. Allow the tree to feel your natural body, relaxed yet alert, free from the burdens you have just released. Stay with this lightness as long as you like. This is the feeling our souls experience when playing through human bodies as Nature wishes us to feel: alive, light and strong. Here you will find the gifts and abilities of a healer.

When you are ready it is time to connect to the branches that stretch out to the upper world, the heavens and Father Sky. If you want, lift your arms upwards. Feel the freedom of the wind and the sunlight. Feel the Spirit of the wind, and the Spirit of the sun. Feel your lightness of being as you strengthen your connection to Spirit. You may have a sense of spaciousness and freedom beyond the limits you have ever imagined. This is how Spirit wills our open minds to experience the restful alertness of creativity. For this moment, experience being a walker between the upper and middle worlds. Here you will find your psychic gifts and abilities.

Feel the connection now to the lower and upper worlds flowing through you. Centre your feelings. You may feel a tingling or vibration anywhere in your body from your fingers to your toes. This is our open mind's and natural body's ecstatic response to our hearts. Our heart centre is the truly beautiful and loving space from where we experience being walkers between the worlds of spirits and souls. Here you will find your inner seer.

In this moment, you are the bridge, the door, the tree linking the lower world of our Earth Mother to the upper worlds of our Sky Father. The Earth is our roots. She grounds us, nurtures us and heals us. The Sky is our branches. He uplifts us, protects us and blesses us. You are as the trunk of the tree, embracing the elements lightly with your outer senses and strongly with your inner sense. You are the love child of Nature and Heaven.

Stay in your heart of all knowing as long as you love to.

When you feel your outer senses beckoning and your inner sense fading know that you are coming back into the middle world. However, you have had a moment with your soul, a moment with Spirit and a moment in your heart. You have found your soul and glimpsed our Earth from your heart.

When you are ready, thank your tree by leaving an offering of food or water for the birds, animals, and others who live around the tree. If you feel like it, set up an altar at the foot of the tree with natural woods and leaves. Know that at any time you can remember this heartfelt experience with your tree. Return here often to feel the tree of life through your newfound long-time friend, your soul.

CHAPTER 7

REMEMBERING OUR SOULS

My past-life workshops are always full. We are fascinated by our past lives and seem drawn irresistibly to have a deeper understanding of where we have come from and who we are. Nearly every culture and tradition has within it a belief system of reincarnation. Ancient Egyptians taught that the human soul is immortal, Hebrew wisdom of the Kabala gives references to reincarnation thousands of years ago and teachings from the Bible include Jesus referring to John the Baptist as a reincarnation of an olden prophet.

Like the Egyptians, ancient Celts were buried with their jewels, clothes and personal belongings for their afterlife journey. During the time of Roman occupation in Britain, Druids still openly taught both reincarnation and fearlessness of death. Pythagoras spent time in Egypt studying reincarnation and told his students about his discovered past life as a warrior at the siege of Troy. As far back as our world's records reveal, seers have always recognized the wisdom of our souls' continuity throughout our many lifetimes here on Earth.

Our souls are immortal. We never die. Living through all our past lives teaches us that we continue on and that life is a circle. The reason why we cannot remember is because we are not able to access our own soul records and soul contracts we made during traumatic times in our lives. Many of us have loved so deeply that we are devastated when we separate from the loved one. We believe we cannot live with out him or her. Our karmic debt, our soul contract, records this and throughout our following lifetimes we repeat and re-experience in relationships what happened in a previous lifetime. This is why we look at soul contracts in all our past lives.

Healing of the past is changing your soul records for many types of trauma. You may now have pain from a past-life injury, wound, or rape, or from when you were murdered, drowned, or burnt. You could be suffering from a love lost centuries ago with whom you made a contract that binds you in this lifetime to your promises of eternal love.

If you have forgotten who you are it is because your behaviours, attitudes and limited beliefs are from the world of selves, from the teachings of unkind ethics and moral judgments that have survived the millennium. You may see the cosmic humour in discovering you were a witch in a previous lifetime and are now a Christian, or the other way round.

When we remember our soul wisdom from lifetime to lifetime, we will know we never die and will have no fear of death. Our souls contain all the information of who we are and where we have come from. Our self sees life through our external senses and practical or impractical thoughts, retaining memories of heartache, fear, hatred, jealousy and anger. Our soul sees with our inner senses and holds all the memories covering centuries of love, passion and adventure. Everything that we once knew and felt that is worth remembering is in our soul's memory, the hall of records, called by some the akashic records. What we do in the present affects us in our future lifetimes, as does our past lifetimes. This is cause and effect, or karma, the natural experience of what we give out returning to us.

We all have many soul mates that we reincarnate and evolve with, and this can be throughout many lifetimes. We have agreed to connect and work together in this lifetime to solve or clear up unfinished business. Our soul mates can suddenly come into our life and cause our self pain and suffering, a repeat performance carried forward from many past lives. This is a soul contract to look at. We review, renew, or cancel our soul records and contracts as we bring them forward into this lifetime.

You can break destructive cycles and free yourself from the soul contract by acting out of love in the present relationship rather than reacting out of fear, and by forgiving rather than repressing your hurt because it will come up for resolution in another lifetime. In this lifetime, we can all complete our karmic debt as if this was our last time on Earth, freeing us to all go Home together as a soul group, as well as to stay here and live naturally together on our Heart's lands.

What are your past life connections with your family and other valued relationships? How do you get on? Are they loving relationships, or love and hate relationships, as in I love my mate but I cannot live with him or her? We recognise our soul mates, the ones who in previous lifetimes we had a loving relationship with. In this lifetime, it may seem totally different. Souls that have been together before in past lives will have a strong attraction to be together. When we meet for the first time, it will feel like we already know one another. It is a familiar feeling, a strong bond that goes beyond space and time, as is the case with May who came to me for a reading here in Egypt.

She has remembered many past lives. Her soul records showed six lifetimes in different Egyptian dynasties that she experienced. She is working though all of her past lives to find the connections to loved ones in her present life. She understands now that her father, husband, and daughters have been with her in previous lifetimes. One of her daughters, June, tells her mother that she will never leave her until the day she dies.

This daughter is reliving her experience from a past life, when as May's daughter in that lifetime, June stayed with her until the day June died at 35. Her daughter in this lifetime now is 35 years old and still lives with her mother. By changing her soul contract from a previous lifetime, June can change the course of her life now. She will then live out a complete life, free from old soul contracts made with others during a past life.

Our souls, spirits, and free wills never change when we pass into the Spirit world between our death and a new birth into a different body. Our body can be either male or female in any lifetime, so imagine if you are born as a boy this lifetime, but your past experiences are that of a girl. Many times this affects our present sexuality. A friend of mine went through a sex change because he felt better as a woman than as a man. He kept saying he felt like a woman in a man's body. In more than 30 of his remembered past lives he was a woman.

The effect of many of our past life experiences are reflected in the circumstances that now surround us and play out in our present day relationships with husbands and wives, mothers and fathers, sons and daughters, brothers and sisters, friends and lovers. Who we are today is the sum total of all of our experiences in all of our lifetimes.

We continue our journey of soul remembrance when we become interested in our past lives. When we illuminate all those mysteries that separate us from the truth of our reality, we discover the purpose for the persons in our present lifetime. We get rid of the negative doubts and feelings from other people's fears and judgments of who they think we should be that is affecting us from lifetime to lifetime.

As children, we remember who we were in past lives, playing out our memories in one form or another. I remember when Winston Churchill died, I was only six years old but I cried all night because I knew him in my heart. Many years later, I was talking to my spiritual dad Dennis one night about past lives. I told him the surprising story of my last lifetime when I was in the Air Force as a pilot. He suggested the reason I was so upset when Churchill died was because I knew him in that lifetime. Interestingly, I have worked in this lifetime for ten years as an Air Stewardess, and I have enjoyed parachuting many times as well.

Who were we acting out when were children? What do we remember of the games we played? I was very much a tomboy, reflecting my previous three lifetimes when I was a man. My adopted father had been in the Air Force and I loved to talk with him about piloting Spitfires. He went along with me, saying to my mother what a great imagination I had.

I did not want to play with dolls and prams. I was climbing trees, beating up the boys, playing cowboys and Indians, knights and dragons. I did not want to grow up. I wanted to stay childlike and remember to play, dance, sing and get up to all the things kids get up to. I did not want to play grown up because that was boring. Grownups all looked so unhappy to me.

I could not feel comfortable being in a brick-built house. It was strange for me because it was not how I remembered living from a time before. I began to realize that all along in the first five years of my life I was seeing visions of native lands and places I had lived. I took trips in my visions to where I now know is Egypt, Rome, North and South America, and even Atlantis.

As a little girl, I was vividly remembering all my past lives while playing them out. I could see them all, so, of course, when it was time for school, it was just too boring compared with what I already knew from my visions. In school I was seeing things all the time. I was made to stand outside the classroom and to put a dunce's cap on. Little did these judgmental adults know that they were actually crowning me with a hat of the witch, wizard, and seer!

Children sometimes come back to the same families when they pass to the Spirit world prematurely. Mothers or fathers sometimes die and come back as children to their own children. Many old souls are young children. As children we remember in part or completely our past lives and will live them out. We then postpone acting out our past memories, often until we are old enough to be free of family ties. Finally, we make a commitment to follow our visions and dreams to different lands, helping us reconnect to the memory of our past lives.

Many of us have stories to tell of sacred sites, houses and landmarks that trigger memories of connections to the land or locale. It can be quite a shock when we get there to find out how it has changed from our memory of it. I travelled to Jerusalem many years ago and was totally confused. Everything had changed. The city was not the same as in my visions of its ancient splendour.

Whether we are aware of it or not, we are drawn back to where we once lived. The only problem is that the fields, woods, lakes and temples have all evolved, eroded, or been modernised. We may be temporarily upset when we come back to our lands after many years, only to find our familiar places torn down in the name of progress.

Why is it that at certain times we know that certain things are going to happen? I believe that this is when we have actually travelled into the timelines through our dreamtime or our visions and then we walk into them in this world. How is it that we go to places and we say that we have been here before? We have, in our past lives.

I had a sudden fear of dying when I was 42 years old. I have seen the Spirit world throughout my life, so I never feared going Home. I knew that my panic could not be from this lifetime, so I went back to my soul's records to find the answer. I discovered my previous lifetime in Italy and sure enough I had died on my own there. In this lifetime I had just separated from Shaun, was working in Italy, and had even considered living there. My past emotions were still echoing in the ancient walls and streets where I returned to remember and heal.

Some of us travel around the world seeking and searching until we find again the land we once lived upon. We feel we have come home to reclaim ourselves and our past lives. We expectantly meet the people and souls we knew in those previous lifetimes. We connect with the goddesses, gods, ancestors and the spirits of the land. Connecting with all our past lives brings us to a completion of who we are today.

Twin flames, twin souls, or split-aparts are one at the beginning of time, created together in divine harmony with our Creator. We are the complement of one another, the divine masculine and feminine. Our twin flame is the other half of our own complete soul. We are together in our first incarnation and come together for our last time on Earth. Beautiful myths of going Home together, two by two, are true.

Many of us go through heart-aching lessons of love before we are ready to meet our eternal twin. We transform soul relationships with many different people into work on our selves to heal old karmic ties. One by one we get rid of all our traumas through our dramatic working, healing, or inspired relationships until we at last experience our wholeness and wellness.

Throughout our lives, we may experience many spiritually dark nights of our hearts, courageously willing our passionate yearning to remember our souls' twin. As Spirit would have it, simultaneously our twins are preparing for the divine reunion on Earth of our hearts, souls and spirits. We feel deep within our very being the rapture of two flames of unconditional love fusing into a holy fire as we remember into life our ancient futures.

Some of us have our twin flames in the Spirit world at this time. We may recognize our twin as our Spirit guide or gatekeeper. Twin flames in all worlds can be of the same sex because within all our hearts is Spirit's harmonious masculine and feminine love. On Earth, meeting our twin flame is unmistakeable. Instantly, we complement and compliment each other. We quietly cheer and uncontrollably tear as seemingly separate fates collapse into our single stellar destiny.

I trust everything is for a purpose. When we begin to see each moment with inner vision, we discover no accidents, coincidences, or mistakes. At long last, we are willing to know our destiny. Perhaps we are even ready to catch the next flight, travel thousands of miles, and find the one person who has felt us for a lifetime drawing nearer.

Ever since I was a little girl, I knew my soul twin was on Earth somewhere. I could feel him. I could see we were connected through a Native American past life, so I started the journey to my beloved very early on. Along the way, I met many men who were my soul mates, but for one purpose or another, we worked though our karma and said goodbye on good terms. Except for one, who remains self-indulgently in a place of fear, mistrust, and ignorance of his loving heart. I pray that one day he will find his way Home.

Every time I went to the USA, I felt nearer to my heart mate. Many psychics and mediums over the years confirmed for me that my eternal husband was somewhere in the New World. I travelled for decades throughout the Americas, finding other amazing soul mates, but not him. Then at the beginning of 2006, just weeks after going through my last death and rebirth in hospital, Spirit told me where I would find him.

As I packed for the journey, my psychic neighbour confirmed that he was in the USA and she could see lots of dragonflies around us. I finished off my last soul contract with James during our last night together. He released my soul to meet the one man who has always and will forever love me. I left Britain next morning, saying to Patricia and many other friends that I was going to meet my husband in Hawaii.

Flying over Hawaii I saw several of the islands, but the Big Island of Hawaii called to me through the mists that surrounded its volcano. I felt home again in a land I had yet to walk upon, and my heart knew it. I landed in Honolulu, staying for a few days with my soul mates Olivia, Mark, and my Spirit daughter Tula. I asked about which of the islands I should visit to get my strength back from the recent surgery.

I was literally going for broke. I had not worked for weeks due to illness, and the snowy winter in the Peak district where I resided kept my beautiful shop desperately quiet. None of that mattered now that my knowing spirits were tour guiding my expectant soul into these island paradises of lush land, fresh air, warm rain and brilliant sun. Over the internet, I booked a last-minute special at a condominium complex on the north shore of Kauai for my final week in Hawaii. For the rest of my month's stay I would follow my heart.

A few days later, I flew off to Maui for two weeks of nurturing healing with Huna and lomilomi massage. I always wanted to see a live volcano. Maui's volcano is not active these days, but the one on Big Island was erupting. Now was my chance. I arranged for a bed and breakfast, and off I flew to the Big Island for the two days I had left before my scheduled week's time-share in Kauai.

I arrived early in the morning on the eastern side of the island, hired a car and drove to the nearby volcano. I was very intent to sing the sacred chant which Nahi gifted me that morning with her Spirit of Aloha. It was a chant to release the old and I was looking forward to burning away the ashes of my fate in the volcano's live fire. My ashes were the hurts, pains and fears of all my lifetimes that came up again for final resolution during my recent hellish death and rebirth.

I arrived at the volcano on the south side of the island and spent the day in prayer and chanting. It was a clearing and a blessing, and I thanked the volcano Goddess Pele for receiving my gifts. I intended to stay that night at the bed and breakfast near the volcano but Spirit knew otherwise. Instead of going there directly after completing my ceremony, I started driving further west. I did not have a map with me, so I said okay, I am off on another magical mystery tour. I felt relaxed as my spirits patiently led my way for the next two hours.

I just kept driving. Every time I investigated the rare side roads, I ended back on the same highway again. I kept asking Spirit where I was being taken. I heard, "Trust." By this time it was late in the afternoon and I was now heading north around the island. I could see the coast and massive lava fields but I was miles from any buildings. I was not going to make it back that night to the bed and breakfast at the volcano.

I said okay, the next road I come to I am going to drive down it, and the first place I come to I am going to stop. During the next few minutes I passed three bed and breakfast signs in front of tropical homes. I did not stop because I knew I was searching for a road. Finally, I saw a turning to the left an instant before I felt my body instinctively snap the car to the left and on to that road. I caught breathtaking glimpses of the ocean a few miles away as the winding road drew me ever closer to it. Suddenly, to my right I saw a bed and breakfast sign. It read, Dragonfly Ranch. I pulled in, parked the car, and made my way up to the entrance.

Standing at the top of the stairs of this spacious, tropical, and eclectic house that seemed to be at one with the enormous Monkeypod trees which nestled beside it, was a well-tanned man dressed comfortably in a sarong, smiling expectantly as I ascended. I looked into his eyes and saw myself. Here was my beloved, my twin flame, my split-apart, my other complete half. I was home.

As we embraced, we both knew there was no more need to search. As he later said to me that night, he felt for the past year that I was coming for him someday from Old Europe. Like me, he had experienced the many initiations of soul remembrance, so he never gave up hope that his twin would join him in paradise. By our third day, we were staying together at the condo on Kauai. That romantic evening, with whales breaching in the distance of our balcony, he asked me to marry him.

I wept uncontrollably at Honolulu airport as we parted a week later. I was heading back to Britain and he was catching the next flight back to the Big Island. Less than ten days later, having shared several astonishingly beautiful e-mails and phone calls, David arrived on a one-way ticket to my homeland. Our engagement was a week later, when we exchanged rings on Valentine's night under a full moon. Three months to the day we met, we were married in Las Vegas.

We needed patience, faith, and courage during this amazing year, especially during the many months we separated around the world to sort out our visas. David now lives and adventures with me, just as we remember doing in our shared past, and know we will be doing in our destined future.

This is what I call love, coming from Hawaii to the heart of Britain in midwinter, one-way. As I write these words, we are in Egypt discovering our many shared past lives here. To remember our lives together, we simultaneously travel the timelines of our souls until we merge. As we look for each other in past and future moments in time, we understand why our one being of two souls has sometimes appeared to separate, even for many lifetimes of seemingly independent work, before remerging.

Seers are able to predict events because we travel the timelines into the future to bring back information for the present. We see the necessary outcome, the fate, of that moment's actions. However, for those who come to us and for ourselves, we change the outcome of future events by changing in the present our understanding of our pasts.

We all have the ability to change our lives, right here and now, by first travelling back into the past and looking at who we were and what we were doing. With this deeper understanding of our souls and selves, we see where we are going in the future and we know why. When we feel happy with what we see, we know the destiny of our souls. When you feel your heart ache by what you see, you have the opportunity to change the fate of your self. You now know the work on your self that your playful soul calls for.

When seers travel the timelines to remember who we are, we go into our hearts for our past, present, and future stories. We see all time in the present moment, knowing our only real experience is the eternal now. For this book, I have traveled on my timelines to the future, looked at the finished book and brought it back chapter by chapter as faithfully as I can.

My experience of traveling to my heart of all knowing, my soul's home of record, is going into a picture gallery with lots of television screens showing my past lives all running at the same time. I am able to look at one screen and describe the images I see and then move on to the next one. It reminds me of the film *Matrix*, where I can watch everything being shown all at the same time.

Our place of all knowing and all understanding, our heart center, is home to every loving memory since the beginning of time and until the end of time. Seers actually never see the traumas of our own or others. This is the vision of selves, since only selves suffer. Instead, we see our souls' compassionate solutions to every problem we have ever had or will have when we did not heed Spirit's wisdom. Traumas appear to me in the records like a paused video. The screen is like a holographic picture. I see a being trapped in a self, frozen in time and kept artificially alive in their traumatised memory.

Seers find unopened gifts left by our souls at the scene of these seeming accidents and bring them back for the person we are reading for to open. We open these gifts of courage and wisdom, and now have the opportunity again to accept them and use them to heal that trauma. All of us experience our all-knowing heart when our bodies die. Many people have shared their amazing experiences of having their lives flash in front of them. To our hearts, this lifetime is a flash.

We who have had near death experiences and have seen our book of life flash in front of us feel we have no choice but to change our lives completely. We have glimpsed our hearts, felt the indescribable comfort of our souls, and knew in that precious moment beyond all doubt our wills to live, our Spirit of life. None of us needs to wait until we are at a point of dying to experience our miraculous hearts.

Every psychic, medium, and seer experiences the hall of soul records from unique viewpoints, just as every Tarot reader gives a unique inter-pretation of the same cards. It is rather like many artists painting the same landscape differently because each one is interpreting it with differing skills, feelings and perspective. When seers connect to our own hearts, we are able to connect to all souls and memories. When helping another, seers connect from our hearts to all hearts of the Heart. We experience no sense of death or time in our hearts, but we can speak of them to help others understand who they are not.

If you have lost touch with where your family has come from, you can access your own soul records to discover long lost relatives, or you can access their soul records. You might even find out you are your own ancestors. Many times when I am in the USA people hear my accent and tell me they have Scottish, English, Welsh, or Irish ancestry, yet they could not trace back exactly where their ancestors came from. I tell them by trusting their seership abilities they will be able to cross all boundaries of time and space and connect with their forgotten ancestors. All of us can connect once again to our seemingly lost ancestry and our hereditary gifts by trusting our intuition and following our instincts.

Seers often confirm the sketchy information we receive in this world with the impartial records from the Spirit world. When I was giving the reading to May, she wanted to know more about where she came from. She did not have any information about her deceased father's ancestry. He came through from the Spirit world to explain that his family was from Spain and originally from Marrakech. May smiled and said that explained many things.

She often thought his dark skin and good looks pointed to either Spain or Italy. What pleased her most was that she had already acted on this information, at the time not realising what she was really doing. For years, May wanted to go to Marrakech. Last year she finally went to complete a vision and a dream of hers. Now she knew that all along she felt a calling to visit exactly where her father's ancestors originally come from.

A couple of years ago I was running a workshop in Jersey on past lives. Among the attendees was Jenny, who had a stutter since she was a child. During the intense workshop, she discovered many things about herself and the partner she was working with. They had not met before the workshop, yet discovered they had a past life together. They went deeper into their past lives and discovered that they had lived in the same town and knew one another. Both also saw that Jenny died by hanging in that lifetime, and the person who hung her was none other than her workshop partner. Jenny now had an explanation for why she had a stutter from birth. The last thing she remembers while hanging was trying to speak and all that happened was a stutter.

Many of you go to the doctor with aches and pains. You have all the tests, nothing shows up, and yet the trauma is still there in your suffering minds and bodies. We release those mysterious traumas by going into our past lives to discover who we once were. By using our divine will we can completely change direction, attitudes and our purpose in our present life. We gain a deeper understanding of why and how our past lives affect us today.

There are many clues to who you have been in past lives that are staring you in the face. What clothes do you love to wear? I am not asking you about your work clothes, although sometimes these are clues if you wear a uniform as a nurse, soldier, fire fighter, or police officer. If you went into a fancy dress shop, or had before you a catalogue of your favourite clothing, what would you choose to wear? Every year I go to

Salem in the USA for Halloween. I love it because there are thousands of people dressed up in costumes that reflect who they were and are. What a pity to wait for one day each year to dress up as ourselves.

What places in the world would you travel to and where would you not go? These give you clues. In the world's history, what period are you drawn to? What films and books do you like to watch and read? Look around your house and you will see many clues as to who you have been in past lives, and who you are waiting to become.

I was guiding a past-life workshop in Cornwall last year. After the journey, I asked who they discovered themselves to be. A gentle man named Paul said he experienced being a Native American and had a wolf with him in his vision. It was his first time connecting to who he was in the past. Yet he was telling his vision to us while wearing an airbrushed tee shirt of a Native American with his wolf.

When we access our past we can review our growth since that lifetime and what we have and have not learnt. We are free to move forward in this lifetime once we have extracted the essence of who we are from those worlds of the past. Very few of us remember all of our past lives or any future ones completely. However, all of us are able to glimpse into our ever-loving hearts to hear our ever-present spirits and remember our everlasting souls.

Exercise 7   REMEMBERING OUR SOULS

Take some time out to connect to who you were in a past life. This gives you clues about your life today. Your dreams and the music you play give you clues, and may trigger memories as well. I have found that travelling to places connects me to my past lives. For me, to walk on the lands is to remember. While writing in Egypt, I am taking time to connect with my past lives here.

This is the time for healing your past. Have a purpose for the journey, an intention. It may be for healing of a trauma from a past life, to meet your twin flame, find your purpose in the present lifetime, or any other special need. Place your wholehearted intention for the journey to fulfill it. Remember the past is still in your present thoughts and emotions.

Find a quiet place so you can lie down with your back comfortably stretched. Totally relax your body by breathing deeply and slowly. Let go of all your everyday thoughts and just breathe. The deeper you drop into your breath, the more answers will be revealed to you.

When you are in a place of peace begin to visualize the tree that you explored in your journey to the other worlds. Get a sense of it, feel it, touch it, become one with the tree. When you are ready step into the tree and begin to breathe with it.

We are about to take a journey to the lower worlds. It is time to call on your gatekeeper to be with you on your journey for comfort and protection. Visualise a staircase leading down into the Earth. When you are ready follow it down, dropping deeper and deeper until you are at the bottom of the stairs, a place that levels out into a hallway. You can see doorways all along the hallway, your entrances to your past lives.

When you and your gatekeeper are ready, you begin to walk down the hallway. You notice numbers over the doors, from 20th century back all the way in time. Stop in front of each door, taking your time to feel whether this entrance is for you. Trust your intuition and your gatekeeper's guidance to know which doorway to step through. Finally, you reach the doorway that feels positive when you ask permission to enter. Take a moment to remember this experience is for your highest good and open the door.

Be aware first of all of your surroundings. Is it night or day, hot or cold? What are you seeing in front of you, what is the landscape? Forest, desert, sea, mountains, buildings, what are you aware of? How do you feel, happy or sad? Look down at your feet, are you barefooted, or wearing shoes or sandals? Look at the clothes you are wearing, what is the style of dress or outfit? Are you a man or a woman? How young are you and how tall? Get a very good look at who you are, where you are, and what you are doing. Are you working, playing or resting?

Start to make your way to where you live. Is your home a house, a hut, a tepee, or maybe a cave? Where do you sleep at night? Become fully aware of who you are here in your past home, in your past life. Do you have a name? What year is it? Ask many questions of your gatekeeper. Why are you seeing this past lifetime? What has it to do with your other lifetimes? The deeper the questions you ask, the deeper your revelations will be. Ask the question that you set as your intention, and allow the knowledge of who you are to flow.

What wisdom from this past life will serve your highest good in your present lifetime? Welcome your past self into being and into your present knowing. Integrate this feeling of who you were from your soul records that surround you. These records are how your vision shows you them, whether as moving pictures, written records, or spoken stories. Now start to change the information in these pictures, records, or stories that you know will not serve you in the future.

It is very much like updating your files in a computer. You get rid of what you no longer need so it will not slow you down. Too many programs from other people really get you confused, such as viruses and mass e-mails that cause ill health to your system. Junk mail is like listening to other peoples do's and don'ts. Take the time for a good, clean update.

Thank your soul for these healing visions. Thank your gatekeeper for being with you and taking care of you. When you are ready go back to the staircase and walk up the stairs to the entrance to your tree. Come back into this world or just drift off to sleep to continue your journeys into other worlds of dreams and visions.

CHAPTER 8

DREAMING OUR SOULS

We arrived at the temple on the banks of the Nile. The sun was about to set and all around us was quiet. We saw no people or houses nearby. Four friends, all knowledgeable and passionate about ancient Egyptian culture, had invited us to join them on a rare adventure.

We were just mooring for the night aboard a faluka, a traditional Egyptian riverboat converted for comfortable sleeping and delightful dining. This was the first evening of our three-day float past an area of Egypt that time has least changed. My soul friends were excited to get off the boat and explore this site that none of us had visited before in this lifetime.

All of a sudden, I felt very tired and needed to lie down and sleep. Usually, I would be the first one off the plane, bus, or boat when adventures lay ahead. I just could not keep my eyes open, so I went to bed while everyone else went off exploring in the last of the day's light. In an instant I fell into a deep sleep.

I was now walking with everybody to a temple, while seeing the whole area of the complex all the way down the banks of the Nile on both sides. I saw the temple partitioned into three ceremonial areas and viewed the many tombs carved into the side of the overhanging rocks along the river. An instant later, I was within a very large field with a distant, massive wall of mud bricks surrounding me. I saw the guardian of the land and asked permission to walk here. I was very aware that I was standing upon sacred grounds of Egyptian ancestors.

Suddenly, I was aware of David inviting me to join everyone for supper. I felt groggy and disorientated as I began recognizing the room while still being aware of the dreamtime. I could still see the details of where I had been and what I had experienced. I started to tell him what had happened and where I had been. He confirmed that the temple they just briefly had the daylight to explore was exactly what I saw.

During our meal I told my friends about what I had dreamt and they too confirmed the details of the first part of my vision. No one remembered seeing the surrounding wall in the distance, so we were eager to find it in the morning. Next day, I fluted to the spirits of the land as the sun gloriously rose over the Nile. We were off early to walk the site, and I spent many hours seeing on Earth what I had already seen in the dreamtime. However, none of us could locate the huge mud-brick wall I had seen so clearly in the dreamtime.

The following day we arrived at another of the several sacred sites we intended to explore. As we walked over the steep ridge of the bank leading to the temple ruins, I saw the enormous mud-bricked wall encircling and protecting the whole complex. As none of us could see where the entrance to the temple was, we split up and headed in opposite directions, following the long wall.

We were moving further and further away from the others, not finding an entrance, when I saw a man walking towards us in the distance. As he neared, I recognized him as the gatekeeper from my dream. We shared our only common Egyptian words of welcome and gratitude. This heart talk was enough. He guided us reverently into the centre of the temple, then back to the entrance. With a knowing smile, he walked off in the direction he had arrived from.

I had journeyed in one dream to two of the several sites we visited during our float through the past. I had an out-of-body experience, a soul journey into the future to see where we were going. I knew the guardian of one temple before we met him. He felt my honour of the ancestors of the land, and guided us within the complex. During my soul flight I was aware of myself the whole time. I knew the experience was real and I was surprised to wake up. It took me awhile to get back in my body properly.

During my sleep I believed that I was completely awake. The colours were so real. I was actively experiencing my happy dream. This is the difference between dreaming our souls and dreaming our selves. Self-dreaming is feeling upset, victimized, or forced into passivity against our wills while asleep. Soul dreaming feels exhilarating as we see our true wills, our souls, effortlessly create our reality while our selves remain dreamless.

We become our souls and find the answers to questions we may only have begun to ask. Our souls dream us to discover our questions, our problems and our quests of the moment. Our souls' gifts in our sleep are visions of our world as seen through our hearts' wakeful eyes. Soul dreams, journeys, and flights come to us whenever we are prepared to let go of our selves for a while.

My lucid dream left a vivid impression on me, and reminded me of my journeys in the Amazon a few years ago. In one of my trips to Peru, I went deep within the jungle. For a full week I purged and purified with sacred medicines and flower baths, tobacco cleansings, sprayings of holy water and light food that cleaned out my insides. These prayerful rituals are the ancient ways of preparing our minds and bodies for drinking the vine of the soul.

For many years I struggled with going on a sacred plant medicine journey. I had accepted the beliefs of others that it was not a good thing for me to do. Finally, I was here within our Earth's lungs, in the midst of unbelievable lushness. I could see, hear, touch, taste and especially smell the richness of life on Earth. I had prayed all week for the journeys to the other worlds. I was ready. That night we all sat together in a ritual hut waiting for the shaman to join us, listening to the sounds of drums and songs throughout the village merging with the amazing noise of the dark jungle.

The energy became electrifying as the door opened for the shaman who was bearing the ayahuasca for our journeying. We waited silently, knowing that this medicine would change our lives forever. We drank a tea of the sacred plant, the vine of the soul, in deep reverence. We listened to the chants sung through the shaman direct from the spirit of the plant. As the billows of ritual tobacco smoke surrounded us I sank into the jungle, leaving my physical body behind.

I became a part of the vast universe until I could no longer feel any difference between the vastness and me. We merged in a burst of fireworks. I became everything and I saw everything. I saw the world of Spirit with my soul eyes wide open, and I gazed from Heaven upon Nature when my soul rested. With open eyes I met the plant medicine teachers, who showed me many visions of who I am. It was all very simple and profound.

I knew peace beyond words, the peace we feel before words of the world enter our minds. The gift of the jungle from the Heart for our souls awakened me in my heart. Since that amazing experience, I have worked with natural medicines from around the world to gain a deeper under-standing of the spirits of these plants. Medicine plants are powerful guides to the energy of the Earth. When we prepare for our journeys, when we know our minds are alert and feel our bodies are relaxed, we connect effortlessly with the ancestors of the land through the plants. We gain insights into our true and beautiful reality.

At the time in my life when I was working with plants for clearer visions, I was trying to control where I went and what I did in the worlds. This was from years of controlled meditation at different colleges. These teachings said I had to do it their way only. During many of my early medicine journeys I saw who I was not. I saw how I had been controlled by society through my parents, school, church, and ultimately, work. The world tried to take away my soul and spirit, and leave me alone with my self. The plant spirits showed me the reality I have seen since a child.

Then my journeys took off. I was free and I flew high above the clouds into the world of bliss and oneness. I felt complete, whole and holy. I had let go of control and was flowing naturally with Nature and Spirit. Our selves do not control our heart worlds. The wind, sun, seas and land are alive. These elements are spirits of our natural cycles of life in Earth and Sky.

I love awakening in my heart, awakening to the very pulse of the Earth and the infinite majesty of the Sky. I understand the wise teachings since the beginning of time: We are living as heart beings, as natural souls, as divine humans of the Earth. Our Earth is the very breath of Our Mother and Our Father. However, to awaken your hearts you do not need to work in the Amazon jungle with ayahuasca, or be with the Native American roadmen doing sacred peyote ceremonies, as I have done.

We experience the same selfless reality through all out-of-body and open-minded adventures, whether by lucid dreaming, medicine journeying, or peaceful meditations. For a blessed moment, we lose our selves in our hearts and find our inner reality. Our spirits will to set us free. Our souls wish to let us play. We fly and do whatever else is beyond the belief and imagination of our selves. I have received songs and played with dragons, fairies, unicorns and many other mythological creatures in the dreamtime. I visit people and places all over the worlds this way.

We evolve with the Earth. What we see today on Earth is a dance of evolution with the moon, the sun, the planets and the stars. During our waking dreamtime, we connect with these heavenly spirits to assist in the natural healing of our planet. Hopi Indians and many other Elders from around the world are feeling the energy of the Earth at all times. They know who we really are. They have the visions of what is happening as well as what is going to happen.

I have traveled into the Spirit world many times to connect with and strengthen my understanding of my destiny on the Earth. While I slept, my soul journeyed and received information about what is happening in the world, and what will happen. Many of us have premonition dreams. Premonitions are future visions, insights and intuitions we receive when dreaming, journeying, or meditating with our souls, day or night.

I woke up very early one morning crying and feeling shaky. I told Shaun I had just been in the middle of an earthquake. I saw buildings, roads and people thrown about everywhere. It was terrible. Then I was in a crashed plane with no door on it and I could do nothing to help all the people. Soon, we heard the news of a Los Angeles earthquake. I already knew this because my soul had taken me there to see, feel and heal. From this experience and others, I know the world has no time to hesitate or waste when many sensitives feel the Earth's energy through our souls.

Mass premonitions become world records of fate when not acted upon in time. Of the major world disasters, the loss of the Titanic was seen more than a decade before it happened. Even a book was written, wherein a ship called Titan hits an iceberg without enough lifeboats. Some people did act on premonitions and cancelled their voyages. We are all able to acknowledge and act upon our premonitions, visions and intuitions. We are all sensitive enough to detect flashes of timely news from our gentle souls and watchful spirits.

Since I have come to Egypt, my dreams have been very intense. I have slept deeply for twelve hours with no breaks or dreamt non-stop. I have also experienced the total opposite of sleep deprivation, when I was not able to sleep during the night and fell into lucid dreaming throughout the day. Often I felt I was awake while I was dreaming. I am staying near the entrance to the Valley of the Kings where the deities, ancestors and creatures forgotten by history rest alongside the remembered souls.

I make offerings to the ancient ones for their blessing that I may rest and play here on this Earth as they once did and that they may work with me now in this world as my Spirit guides. I asked the guardian and protector of dreams to share with me the wisdom and insight of these lands in my dreamtime.

As I have walked upon the land and worked with the deities at the different temples I have gained a deeper and more profound under-standing of dream incubation. My dreams have played a very important part of my initiation into these ancient lands. Each night I have asked for healing from the land and every day I have received healing in many ways.

Egyptians built temples called Serapeums, named after Serapis, god of dreams. They were located throughout Egypt where the people would come to receive answers to questions. In these temples dream incubation was the sacred art of honouring ancestors within the temple walls and of appreciating the surrounding land.

When I visited the temple of Dendra near Luxor for the first time many years ago, as soon as I stepped inside the gates I wanted to lie down. I could not stop yawning, so I sat in the temple and closed my eyes. Off I went into my heart worlds. I connected to the dreamtime of the ancestors of the land and to the blessed souls whose gifts were received on the sacred altar in this ancient home of goddesses and gods. Recently, I discovered that Dendra was built as a dream temple and realised why I had so strongly felt the instinct to rest.

In ancient cultures dreaming was divine inspiration, a gift of Heaven. They understood that dreams come as clear messages from Spirit or as symbols from our souls requiring interpretations by dream oracles. Early Christian communities had dream prophets, or interpreters, and the Hebrews incubated dreams to receive divine revelations. The Romans had dream interpreters with them when they went into battle, as did many other ancient cultures. Generals visited the dream temples before embarking on matters of importance to gain guidance and wisdom.

The Native American way of vision questing was to contact their ancestors in the dreamtime. They would fast, spend time in isolation and experience sleep deprivation to receive visions from the Spirit world. Aboriginal people call our Earth walk the dreaming, the all-at-once, whereby the past, present and future co-exist as one moment. Like seers, they experience timeless reality. They walk their song-lines into being and become one with Nature and Spirit. They are dreaming awake the true understanding of life on Earth.

Intentional dreaming, trance journeying and prescribed meditation are ancient soul-seeking practices. Early sacred cultures on Earth and later spiritual and therapeutic communities in the West understood the transitory or trance nature of hypnotic healing. Initiates, believers and patients reached states of surrendered self-will through dancing, fasting or exercising and chanting, praying or affirming.

These transient or passive ways of curing our selves are healing glimpses of our awakened seer hearts. Under self-hypnosis you may be having a wonderful dream, journey or meditation, when suddenly your worldly self says, "Hold on a minute you cannot do that, it is impossible," and you wake up from your heart worlds of spirits and souls.

I dream, journey and meditate so readily because my outer mind switches off. I just let my self go and let my soul come. Our soul, dream body or shamanic double is called the astral body because during sleep our soul rests peacefully with the stars, the astral world. We see the whole truth when we go beyond the boundaries of what we believe to be true.

To intentionally dream, we ask Spirit and our soul to solve our problems in the dreamtime. Our wishes are fulfilled before we ask and the information we need is available already in our dreamtime. We step out of our middle world's clock time and mapped space into the infinity of our soul world, our world of happy dreams. We travel into the past, the present and the future and then rest in the world of eternity, Heaven, with all-knowing spirits. We all have a daily and effortless opportunity to refresh ourselves with our souls and spirits.

During dreamless sleep, we renew the energy used up by our selves and heal our bodies as we rest our minds. When the mental state we are in when we go to sleep is peaceful and relaxed our dreaming will be peaceful and relaxed. If we go to sleep stressed our dreams will reflect what has stressed us during the daytime. When you go to sleep at night, you can ensure your rest by remembering your protection.

At night, do you just get into bed, close your eyes and go off to sleep? This is very much like going on a magical mystery tour blindfolded. You have no clue where you are going, who is driving you, when you are going to get there and if you are going to be safe. Will you like it when you get there, will you get food and drink? Will you enjoy the experience? How and when will you get back? Most of us would not travel like this in our waking state.

When you go to sleep, you can plan your trip into the heart worlds. I get excited when I intend my soul adventures for the dreamtime. What will I do tonight? Where will I go and whom will I meet? I love going to ancient sites and sleeping there because some of them are sites of dream temples. I just want to lie down and journey on the timelines. I go into the past to meet the ancestors of the land, then into the present time to find out why I have travelled there, and then into the future to see my destiny. My soul dreams me as I dream my soul.

Exercise 8 DREAMING OUR SOULS

You can create your own dream temple, a sacred space for sleeping, in your bedroom or a small room just for you. You can decorate your room with stars on the ceiling. I have created my dream temple, even with a skylight to the stars. If you can, sleep outside underneath the stars and moon, just as we did in our past lives at the dream temples. You may even be able to spend time on a vision quest out in Nature.

Wherever you sleep, make it as naturally peaceful as possible. If natural quiet is not possible, play some Earth-honouring music or recorded natural sounds that take you into the dreamtime. Imagine how it would have been all those hundreds of years ago and create the atmosphere with incense and candles that are in safe containers should they burn all night.

Choose a perfect night. A good time for soul dreaming is around the dark of the moon or during an evening when you are not working the next day. This is your time for rest, so keep the evening clear with no phones or people visiting you. Have a long bath or shower and eat lightly. To have the best opportunity for lucidly dreaming your soul, give your mind a day off from telly, newspapers, radio and gossip. If a meditative day is not your preference, then sing, play, compose or listen to your favourite relaxing music.

Either have a journal and several pens for recording all your dreams or use a tape recorder to speak all the information straight away. I use a tape recorder because often I am not awake enough to get my thinking left-brain into writing. I can speak into the tape, go straight back to sleep and when I am fully awake I will write it my dream journal. I find this way so much easier. Another option is to have paper and sharpened coloured pencils to draw what you experience as rapidly as you can.

It is time for you to go to your place where you will be dreaming. Bring your journal or tape recorder. Light your candles and burn your incenses to create your sacred space. Write down on a piece of paper what it is that you wish to solve or do in the dreamtime and place the paper under your pillow. Lie down, allow your body to relax and breathe. We are going to the place between waking and sleeping, between your outer and inner mind, and between your outer and inner body. We are intending to go into the roundabout of our worlds, where the thinnest of veils dissolves between selves, souls and spirits.

When you are ready, see in front of you an ancient dream temple. It feels very familiar to you. At the entrance are your guardians of the dreamtime. They are here to help, protect and assist you in your journey into and between the worlds. You may already know them, or you might have seen them in the dreamtime before but not have recognized them. They come forward and greet you with open arms. You feel safe and well.

As you enter into the temple, you see in front of you a small courtyard. You walk into it and you see a beautiful fountain in the middle. You look up and see the stars shining brightly above you. This is your sacred dream sanctuary from where you will journey tonight. You look around, and you are amazed to find your favourite bed for sleeping. Is it a lovely grass area, your sacred rug or magic carpet, your childhood bunk, your deluxe air mattress, or your magnificently cushioned hanging bed suspended from four sturdy trees you planted years ago?

It feels inviting, so you go over and sink into your comfy warm bed. Once you are lying down, you look up into the stars and ask the question three times that you want solved then release it and let it go into the heavens.

It is time to journey into the stars. Feel like you are lifting off into the sky. You are getting lighter and lighter as you sink deeper and deeper into your bed. You start to feel as if you are waking up, but you feel safe and relaxed so you remain awake in your sleep. As you lift higher and higher, all of a sudden you feel as if you have wings. You look around and notice you are flying into the night sky. You are alive, you are awake and you are free. It is now your choice to go wherever you want to go. Allow yourself to soar, to travel, to explore with your playful soul.

When you are ready, fly into the roundabout and glimpse into the worlds as you circle by them. Who are your gatekeepers to the upper, lower and middle worlds? Take a moment during your flyby to hover near the entrances. What do you see and how do you feel as you gaze through the eyes of your playful soul into Nature, through the eyes of your wise spirits into Heaven and through the eyes of your self into your daily life.

When you wake up from your journeying, immediately record your impressions either on tape or paper. As often as you can, continue this journey. Remember to rest and play here in the dreamtime. Take the piece of paper from under your pillow and place it on your ancestral altar during the daytime.

Notice the difference between your dreams. Are they premonitions, lucid dreams, meeting with your Spirit guides or out of body experiences? Sometimes they will not have any meaning until you study your pictures, read your journal or listen to your tapes at a later time. Have dream meetings with friends or arrange to meet with your beloved at an arranged location in the dreamtime.

If you chose to write or tape your dream, remember to sketch any symbols, pictures or places you wish to recall later. Research your guardians of the worlds if you do not recognize them. Draw or obtain a picture of them if it is available. Write down what places you visit each time you go to your dream temple. Are you having happy dreams?

CHAPTER 9

SENSING OUR HEARTS

In our infinite wanderings as souls in Nature while peacefully resting as spirits in Heaven, we became quite familiar with the joy of playing with the Earth's treasures, Her natural life forms. We experienced the enchantment of Her day and night suns as regal trees, the glee of Her shifting winds as kingly birds, the delight of Her heaving seas as queenly creatures, the pleasure of Her abundant lands as mighty animals, and the charm of Her gracious Spirit as fairies, dragons, and divine humans.

There was one instant when divine human beings experienced something different from our eternal happiness. One of us had a strange experience, a mysterious need that no other soul ever had. Because souls knew all worlds as one reality we had no need or knowledge of otherness. Until this moment, we all felt blessed at rest and blissful at play. Now someone experienced a mystery, an unknown instant. Before we knew it, other sensitive souls also felt this instant of unhappiness. To this soul group the experience felt neither spirited nor soulful, neither restful nor playful, neither blessed nor blissful. It felt mysterious.

Souls had always felt and known only the happiness and harmony of Spirit. None of us had the ability to rest or play with a mystery or to choose between the unknown and the known. We have Great Spirit's wisdom, so there is nothing unknown and no mystery to us. We have all our Goddess' grace, so there is nothing to need or choose at all. We had everything in the universe to play through and nothing in the universe to disturb our rest. Yet one lost soul, and now others, somehow felt an instant of unnatural effort, the hard work of trying to make sense of a mystery.

Without choice, souls that know, feel and love all things can not happily co-exist with a need that comes out of nowhere. In the same instant, we felt the strange experience of separation from the unhappiness, the mystery, the unknown and senseless need. Time stood still until we felt again the happiness we already knew by Heart, as if for the first time.

In time, we who rested and played together as divine humans received a world of opportunity like none we had ever experienced. Our gift was a mysterious world of humans who struggled with the unknown, with doubts and questions. These strangers did not rest like us in the upper world of Spirit, or play with us in the lower world like our real friends, our whales, owls, fairies and dragons. They were separated souls, lost spirits called selves who had changed from the divine beings we had but an instant ago rested and played with in love.

These selves did not relax and play with the human bodies as we do. They worked. They experienced an unhappiness that we could only imagine. From the moment they had separated from us, their soul mates, human beings felt lost in our natural bodies and at home in their confused and unnatural minds.

These selves were unhappy with their unnatural human bodies because they used parts of their bodies for working and kept unused parts for worrying. A part of the formerly natural body, the brain, expended much effort. It now housed most of the self's worries about work. The rest of the body parts unused to work were where selves kept worries that were more effort than they were worth working on at the time. Our natural bodies experienced all this unnatural effort as trauma.

We were unable to know the selves' unnatural homes of mystery, their dispirited minds, because they filled these up with made-up questions that caused unhappiness to their bodies. These human beings invented names for their experiences of traumatic work and dramatic worrying in their made-up world. In their confusion, they lived near-daily these near-death experiences.

During that instant of the separation of souls, our play and rest through some human beings continued spiritedly and soulfully as ever. We remained happy souls, without confused minds and traumatized bodies. We knew the unhappy strangers had to be imaginary, an illusion and a dream, because in our known worlds and reality only perfect happiness exists. Except for an instant ago, when without ever leaving, happiness miraculously returned to us. We could not get to know these suddenly mysterious souls because unhappiness is a mystery to all-knowing souls.

We discovered one familiar place in these now unfamiliar self-occupied bodies where we could still experience our soulfulness with our separated souls. The very centre of the heart space of all human bodies was happily unaffected by working or worrying, the life or death situations of seemingly soulless human beings. Instantly, we knew where to place our gift we had just received that we never felt without because we always felt it within. We might not be able to know these lost souls, but we could still share with them the miracle of our happiness. In one instant, we received a miracle, and in the next instant, we give it away. We dream with our selves in the centre of their hearts where our souls feel every happy moment from our real worlds.

We love the opportunity, however brief, to share with our selves the happiness that never left us, yet once returned. We know this strange world of separated sensitive souls will vanish as instantly as it came into being the moment the last selves open their minds to the happiness in our Heart. This dream of a working world only exists by the self-effort and soul sacrifice needed to keep separate the unknown from the known, their unnatural thoughts from our natural feelings and the mystery of misery from the miracle of love. We love our selves completely by not pretending to make real the unknowing misuses of their minds and unfeeling abuses of their bodies.

We can only imagine the effort and unhappiness endured by our selves because the human companionships of spirits and souls with selves remain silent. They listen almost endlessly to the unasked questions called doubts and the unanswered questions called beliefs that make up their minds. We do not mind. Our spirits mind us as we continue to create and recreate awhile through divine human beings. We forgive and forget the unhappy separateness of our lost souls while playing within the heart space of self-distorted human bodies. By our very presence, these bodies become our bodies because they are beautiful in our forgiving eyes.

Our selves invented tales of their instant's adventure into the unreality of the first mystery, the primal unhappiness and the original separation anxiety. Yet even our divine Parents seemed not to have Their typical infinite patience to listen to these sad, made-up stories. Our selves are spending what feels like to them the rest of eternity making sense of their lives of work and nonsense of their deaths of worry.

To make the history of its nonexistent world more believable, our selves made up tricks to ignore, repress, deny, rationalise, analyse and project away their mysterious last instant of remembered happiness. That memory is not in their minds because that instant birthed their selves from souls. We lovingly rebirth the undying memory of miraculous happiness within the lost soul hearts of their overworked bodies and on into their dispirited minds.

Selves became cleverer with their unknowingness by making up problems for themselves and their world. Some dreamt up multiple questions needing a separate spirit to work on each problem. Some extended themselves into many lifetimes with unfinished business and nonexistent problems that required ages before their inevitable abandonment. We enjoy these opportunities to experience many spirits in a single self, and many selves as a single soul. Only selves think up lifetimes and unnaturally task their human bodies to sense their time to toil and their time to die. Natural bodies sense life, the time-outs of rest and the all-the-time-in-the-world feeling of play.

We make no effort to create and play in minds. Unhappy dreams are unnatural to us. Troubled minds block our whispered Spirit voices by the effort of some rational or irrational objection. Untroubled minds of newborn souls open their innocent ears to us and remember our Heart, our Hearth and our Home. They remember what we never forgot. They remember who we all really are: effortless, open-minded, happy children of all ages. Our never lost souls are our innocent babes who have not yet met the selves who impose upon our tender hearts their middle world lessons that stress our newborn minds and distress our awakening bodies.

Divinely human beings continue to happily rest and play with us in the upper and lower worlds. We share our infinite wisdom and eternal love through open heavenly minds and friendly natural bodies. We remember our happy hearts when we go off to the schools and jobs where souls get weary from the effort of it all. We play awhile in this world as spirited workers of miracles while resting soulfully in the Heart of all worlds. We are the Earth-gazing seers and Sky-dancing lovers.

Seership is the foundation of our collective human story because we all have been, will be, and are now the seers. Seers walk between the worlds of selves, spirits and souls. We weave the worlds together with our willingness to live from our hearts. We are able to blend the dimensions of our minds, bodies and hearts. We trust unquestioningly the personal mental and physical power emanating magnetically from our passionate hearts. We live in gratitude and harmony with Nature and Heaven.

Our truly Great Seers are the One and All of Heaven and Nature, Who re-create in earth and sky, with rain and sun, all the wisdom and love within Their creative Heart. The Sky and Earth have been home to our human spirits and souls for millions of years. We have all experienced through many lifetimes Nature's cycles of movement, change, rebirthing, and stillness. Seers remain aware of Nature's wholeness. We relax our natural bodies to sense the presence of Spirit, within and without. We also rest our bodies in perfect trust throughout our dreamtime, out-of-body, and near-death adventures.

I remember many years ago having an amazing lucid dream that foretold my destiny and explained to me what seership is all about. I was standing in front of a very big house that was going up in flames. People were running past me into the building. I shouted to them that the house was on fire and not to go that way, but they ignored me and still went into the burning house.

I turned around and started walking away from the fire. As I did, some of the people who were running past me stopped and without me saying anything to them they started to walk away with me. I arrived at a bridge and everybody with me started to cross over into the next world. They were happy and full of joy.

Yet thousands of people kept running past me. Again, some turned around and crossed the bridge without saying a word. I spoke with Spirit and asked the meaning of the dream. Spirit explained to me that I could only help those who asked for help. The self drives us into the burning building, the place of self-destruction. When we listen to our souls we cross over from a self-experience to our soul experience. Those crossing the bridge with me were souls going Home in this lifetime of their own free will without having to die first on Earth.

Spirit answers our willingness to bridge the worlds with the gift of seeing through the veil of death. Spiritual vision comes to us from deep within our hearts. This is where our truths live in unity with all truth. Our hearts remind us how to read scrolls of human lives and foretell events. Seers talk with a person while simultaneously travelling backwards and forwards in his or her unique story. We are inwardly sensitive to the effect of trauma in this or any other lifetime of the person. We stay relaxed while paying attention.

We walk between the worlds to discover the seemingly inexplicable cause of their present suffering. We see the frozen reactions of their mind and body to trauma. We receive healing thoughts from Spirit to soothe their emotional unease. Their mind's wellness releases their body's attachment to any illness or disease manifesting in this moment. As we reconnect to our heart's eternal memory of grace and ease, miracles happen.

Seership is a passionate trust in the Holy and Great Spirit. I am writing this book to help you strengthen your trust. You can be healed by your courage to remember your divine nature. A seer heals and is healed by our all-powerful hearts. Homes are happy when a seer is consulted because

Spirit gives the divine energy of love to the seer in the perfect form at that moment for the whole family's needs. We trust Spirit to bring us visions that help us remember and understand the one Source of the seemingly many worlds.

A change in consciousness is occurring in our world today. What I see is that we have come to a time in our human evolution when we are ready again to create the future of our cherished dreams. The radical change in human destiny anticipated for 2012 is already happening. Spirit has told me since I was a little girl that 2012 is not the end of the Earth. Instead, it is the time available for a collective change of consciousness in the world.

When we change our own lives, we change the lives of everyone and everything we know by heart. By remaining aware of the interconnectedness of souls and spirits in our daily lives, we in turn affect all the worlds in this one universe. We make a difference by being responsible to our souls and responsive to our spirits. We are willing to change our way of acting and thinking to serve our heart's memory of human evolution. We remember our unique and divine presence in the universe, and help others remember who we all are. We teach what was and may again be taught in the homes, schools, churches and temples.

We know, sense and feel the truth when we access it. Seers reveal truths to satisfy believing minds. We offer love to heal the traumas of fearful bodies. We commit ourselves to staying connected to our hearts of wisdom and compassion. Our spiritual experiences remind us of the eternal love that Spirit gifts to us everywhere in the universe. We communicate with relations resting in the Spirit world and playing in the soul world. We travel into the future to perceive the events that will occur based on this moment's momentum. We travel into the past to understand the cause of our inevitable present moment.

Seers are sensitive. Knowledge of future events arouses our willingness to act and passionately live out our destinies. The past affects us differently. We need do nothing about it because no new effects or experiences from the past are possible. We are present as witnesses to the timeless reality of the Spirit world. We see our ancient future instead of a mirage on the horizon of time.

For mediums and psychics, contact with spirits occurs second-hand through a Spirit guide. Seers have Spirit guides and helpers as well, but we also communicate directly with the Source of our one shared and eternal life. If I want a Spirit guide who works with astrology, that is who comes, and if I want assistance with modern medicine, then they will assist me. The appearance of separateness in the Spirit and soul worlds is to simplify our understanding of reality to our selves. Yet reality is seamless. Selves do not understand wholeness and wellness because this reality of connectedness is beyond their separate, secret and unhealthy beliefs.

I get my energy directly from the Source. It is a personal positive power that feels good to share. I have no need for any lesser or greater power because my heart is full of Spirit's mighty gentleness. No one needs to go to anyone else to contact the Creator. If I want to talk with the Spirit world, I do not phone up someone to speak for me because I want to speak to Spirit myself. I have a 0800 number to my heart, and so do you.

Our soul is a star waiting to be born and soon discovered by others. How many of us are waiting for somebody to see who we truly are? I see hundreds of people whose souls and spirits are begging me to tell their minds and bodies to disconnect from their selves and reconnect to who they really are. Souls feel the presence of life through all natural bodies. When working with the worried and wearied, seers sense the spirits of the absent-minded and the souls of the functionally disabled.

Have you ever wondered why today, as well as in the past, we journey to high places and secluded mountain caves to find great seers? The closer we get to our time for greater wisdom, the stronger our magnetic energy becomes to attract the reflection of the seer within us that we are prepared to find mirrored on Earth. Spirit does not need seers and saints to shout from the rooftops as to who they or we are. God and the Goddess are our knowingly silent Partners.

Silence is helpful when we go within and connect with our soul. It unlocks the doors of greater and deeper mysteries and reveals our inner vaults of priceless wisdom. I find a great oneness whenever I enter into the world of Spirit. It is so peaceful that my sensitivity effortlessly expands beyond my body's normal range of sensing.

Seers appear to be reclusive or solitary, saving rather than spending time with Nature or in Heaven when the noise of the modern world is all too much. We are leaving the cities and towns because we are sensitive to the vibrations of the joyous energy of spirits as they attend their loved ones in these populated areas. Our ancestors and departed loved ones practice the same degree of patience and enthusiasm when greeting us in this world as they attained during their personal Earth walks.

So we move to the country to ground ourselves back into the familiar nurturing energy of the elements. Our minds and bodies surrender to our heart's perfect sense of living in Nature and Heaven while on Earth. We know there is no place to go or hide where the Spirit world is not, yet we also know of quieter places on Earth where our sensitive souls can rest in peace with the Great Mother for a short while. Selves shy away from our sacred sites because we are in clear view of our all-seeing Heart.

Seers travel as messengers to and from the Heart of the worlds. We deliver our divine messages of hope and comfort to the seemingly dark places in this world where souls are ready for release from the shadows of divine ignorance and man-made shame. I see light within and surrounding every single person. Seers detect in the light of our minds and life of our bodies what is in all our hearts. We track through time and space to access the information that is within our open hearts.

Seers become one with Spirit and Nature as simply as we surface into the air from an underwater dive, or return to the sun from a shady nap. In our ancient times and places on Earth we placed the Sun in the centre of our consciousness. Star gods and goddesses have never left our skies or our hearts. They are our eternally vigilant light bearers, our solar deities of inner vision who acknowledge us as their seers. The divine flames of Spirit are forever the molten core of our inner being, erupting as souls like fiery volcanoes of joy from our happy hearts.

Nature nurtures us with warming fire from our stars. Heat is Nature's gift for our comfort, re-creativity and enjoyment. We sense variations of energy from the Sun's fire as heat, light, electricity and magnetism. Energy's purpose in the universe is to express life. All wisdom of Heaven and Nature is gifted us for the mere willingness to yield our minds to the utter passion of the universe.

Do you see the unspeakable beauty surrounding us when our telltale tears for a time keep its truth in our minds? From the very moment of our conception we are the perfect life forms to bring the truth and beauty of the universe onto this Earth. Seership is the birthright of every soul living today on this amazing Earth. What you see in Nature is a reflection of who we are in Heaven. The unnatural world wherein we work and worry is a refection of who we are not. We are not our selves.

Seers know that a free will is one that entrusts the mind to our heart's keeping as effortlessly as flowers open to the sun. How many times have you said, "I already know that"? Listen to what your heart is telling your mind with your body's own lips. We become visionaries of tomorrows when we lay our yesterdays to rest in perfect peace.

Seers remain clear of self-judgments or self-criticisms. We are worry free and spiritually generous. We silence our busy minds and speak from our patient hearts. We redevelop our left and right brains to function as a whole. We remove fears and traumas within our being and become well. We express our spiritual nature as willing old souls with beginner's ready minds and able Earth bodies.

Spirits and souls have answers and solutions. Intuitions and instincts are from our hearts because they are answers to mind questions and solutions to body dilemmas. Our inner knowing is available every moment for our body's natural responses. Our instincts are our soul experiences encoded as genetic information.

We do not remember or plan our senses. We only feel them as they occur now. We know our natural body feelings as instincts. This is our body's wisdom, solutions to our health and happiness. Outer minds think only of problems, practical or impractical. Intuitions are good ideas because they are true. What we believe are good ideas are not always good ideas in reality, just to the selves who energize beliefs with effort.

It is effortless to be present with Nature or Spirit. Work is required to pay attention to this world of selves. It takes effort to read newspapers, balance checkbooks, keep appointment diaries, make lists, shop for next week's anticipated needs and plan the future.

Gifts from our hearts are amazing talents, amusing play, brilliant insights and natural instincts. From selves, gifts are tricks, lures and cons. Throughout the universe only selves are not harmonious. They are selfish. Selves take things personally, but things are for sharing and appreciating. When we take personally our intuitions and instincts, they become selfish thoughts and emotions.

Selves capture practical thoughts in their minds and trap emotional upsets in their bodies. All this effort brings artificial life to worry and trauma. Thus, effort is the unnatural death of peace and harmony. When you distrust the universe or worry about the world, you have no choice but to react angrily and waste your precious efforts. Busy minds want more time and fearful bodies need more space. Our minds and bodies are happiest when our heart's knowing is flowing.

Exercise 9   SENSING OUR HEARTS

Great Spirit and Mother Nature cannot give us anything until we are ready to receive. If we believe that we do not deserve our gifts or we are unwilling to accept the gifts, then they will seem to be kept from us. Yet no matter what state of willingness or readiness we feel ourselves to be in, we are always able. All the power, passion, wisdom and abilities that we can use will flow to us when we are attuned to receive them. We express our gratitude by manifesting our gifts in this world, working from our hearts with complete trust.

We all have unique spiritual sight, just as we have different physical eyes. We can develop our inner Spirit sensitivities by becoming more conscious of Nature's forces outside us. Our physical eyes and our other outer senses provide us with the opportunity to observe carefully Nature's stillness and cycles. To see with our inner eye or insight, we similarly become quiet observers of the Spirit world. We remain alert but unaffected by what is revealed to us. We trust the visions and images that Spirit shares with us.

The Spirit world is around us all the time, so whether we are in the forest or in an airplane we can still feel our heart's connection to the eternal. All life since the beginning of time exists simultaneously and forever. Forms come and go, appear and disappear, yet life is eternal. Seers live with the seemingly dead, touching them as they touch us. We give breath to their ever-ready messages.

Let us become familiar with the profound depth of your own inner sensing, your heart's sense. In this exercise, we will create the simple conditions for feeling our blessedness without and within. Throughout the exercise, briefly cover or close your eyes whenever you are ready to go more deeply into the moment. Go to your sacred space where you have set up your ancestral altar, or to another altar of your choice out in Nature.

Sacred space always surrounds us without and within. Our bodies are temporary temples for communion with Nature and Spirit. Pause to honour your own sacredness by taking the time now to relax in a protected place of peace and quiet. From this holy place, you will enter a world that you may not have explored since the nearly forgotten days of your childhood wonder.

Nature's primary school teachers are the elements. They have been with us since the Earth was ready for our human habitation. The elements have already helped you build and use your ancestral altar. With their help we are now ready to remember more. Ensure that nothing will disturb you during your sacred time. Get comfortable. Either sit or lay down and if you have a blanket wrap it around you. Begin to allow yourself to feel free again. With no thoughts, feel the oneness with all that is around you in this holy moment.

Firstly, we will connect with the element of fire. Usually the most accessible and natural fire element is the sun. I always acknowledge the sun, even when it is cloudy or raining. If your sacred space today is outdoors, feel now the heat of the sun. Become one with the heat of the solar fire. If you are indoors or if it is night-time, then light a candle and gaze into its light. Feel the living flame. Let it bring back your memories of huddling around a fire to keep warm with your friends, family or ancestors. Allow this warmth to rekindle your inner fire, your heart's desire.

We next connect with the water element in your moment of reverence and reverie. Drinking a cup of tea, soaking in a bath, floating in the sea, or sitting awhile next to a pond or on a riverbank are all means of remembering water's familiar relationship to your emotions. No matter how you choose to use your outer senses in this moment to relate with water, your inner knowing is ever aware of the flow of life within changing forms. Just as your physical heart pours new blood into your precious body with every beat, our spiritual hearts perpetually pour new life from one apparent container to the next. Take time now to participate in the flow of your life and all life.

We next remember the earth element. All of our outer senses have a special relationship with this element, so taking the time to feel the Earth is our "second nature". Sit, stand or walk relaxed yet alert. Without effort, feel the Earth beneath your body. For all your days, with eyes opened or closed, in sickness and in health, know as seers do that the Earth ever supports us. Let your heart rejoice to its content.

Becoming aware of the element of air is easy. Just try not to, even for an instant. The element of air is a masterful reminder of our connectedness with one another and all life. Wherever you are for this sacred time of reflection, take a breath as if it is your first one. Breathe your next breath as if it is your last one. Forget for a moment what your mind knows of oxygen, nitrogen, smog, fog and vog. Feel what your heart knows about this glorious gift of breath. And breathe.

Then merge these four elements together as one experience. Feel them flow into you and around you, nurturing and supporting you. Within and without are the earth, water, fire and air. Let go of time. Be aware of the life around you and inside you. Make a connection with every bird, tree, animal, and blade of grass. If you are indoors, notice everything about the sacred space you have created with these simple elements. As seers, we know there is really no separation between anything. Even these elements are expressions of something simpler.

Souls are simple without being simpler. To Spirit, all elements of Nature are one. In our hearts, all senses are one. Seers live from the heart and sense All as One. We see Spirit in every rock and leaf. We feel Nature in each ray of sunlight and every breeze. We are sensitive to the fact that we are spirits and souls having a human experience. We are naturally amazed with the grace.

Take time each day to be sensitive to your heart, to thank your natural surroundings and to awaken your inner seer.

CHAPTER 10

SEEING OUR EARTH

Remember the thrill of being in the moment during a sporting event, like running or swimming toward some distant goal, when you see yourself simultaneously at the goal in record time as you bound or stroke towards it? In that moment, we saw our destiny and allowed our bodies naturally to fulfill it. Afterward, we tried to explain how we already felt what we would accomplish. We never forget those moments when we really knew our bright future and good fortune.

Our soul knows for all time what we would accomplish when we listen to our all-knowing hearts. We experience the all-time visions of seers and know our destiny. We experience the stillness, the single-pointed focus, the Spirit vision of our minds and the free, energetic, natural motion of our bodies. We experience our souls' resting in the eternity of Heaven while playing in the infinity of Nature. Our hearts of all knowing feel this wonderful state all the time and here is the place seers come from.

Seers take responsibility into our own hands and become the masters of our own destinies. Our future depends on our willingness and readiness to recreate whatever Spirit has created for our destiny. We intend our future with every action, whether selfish or heartfelt. Many bestselling books and charismatic speakers promote positive thinking and visual-ization techniques. To fulfill our own destiny, however, we have to be as hollow as a bone, a Nile reed, or as Krishna's flute.

Fate is not our freedom and freedom truly is our destiny. Fate is travelling through life as passengers. Destiny is getting into the driver's seat. There are always two roads to travel for every human being during our Earth walk. The seer within us all is able to decide which path is most natural and effortless. When someone comes for a reading and asks to know their destiny, the seer can view the roads in front of that person as if from a hot air balloon and can advise them about these roads. If you take the fate road this will happen but if you release control of your life energies from all selves including yours, your soul and spirits unfold your destiny.

Awakened seers help people make best choices for themselves. We are all here on Earth to remember our natural birthright of awakening our inner seer. We get in touch once again with the divine. Let us be the visionaries of our destiny and not let fate take us for a ride. Many of us are now making choices that free up our will, our desires and our passions so they may be reborn as the powerful gentleness of happiness.

When love is the power of what we do and when we come from our hearts in all we say, we are not controlled by anything traumatic from the past nor to come. We fully realise that we are born as divinely human beings and understand that the selves we become in this lifetime are not our true nature. Our selves think they determine what we do and say in this world. Yet our souls know what makes us happy to do and say in all worlds. Seers are on Earth to encourage selves to make decisions that reflect our all-knowing hearts.

As mere children, most of us were forced to surrender our innocence to the world's unhappiness. That original surrender of our heart's desire is our welcome to this world. We evolve our selves in each lifetime as we reconnect to the universe of Nature and the Source of all life. Seers bring our souls and spirits into this unnatural world and unreality of selves. We receive the knowledge of spirits and pleasure of souls, allowing their free flow into ourselves. We live through our hearts and unite with Heaven and Nature when appearing to work in this middle world. Seers are rich, whether or not we are moneyed.

There is much myth and misunderstanding about how seers bring our gifts into this world. I have perused a couple of seership books written in the 1890 – 1930 eras, which appeared to only address men. Some state that passion and sex dim the gifts of a seer, that a seer must feed and cleanse the body properly and that all thoughts and impulses must be controlled. While helpful for some beginning and advanced seers, none of this is required by our hearts.

Seers, angels, Spirit guides, and Nature through Her plentiful signs do not control selves or souls, nor tell people their fortune or fate. Seers access a record of every thing and every thought that has occurred on this Earth and beyond since the beginning of time. Seers know what is perpetual and what is momentary. We hold both truth and illusion in our vision, and return life to the truth by releasing all energy bound to the illusion.

We see the divine wholeness and completeness in all beings, not separateness. We bring unity to the seeming dualities of spirits and souls, intuition and instincts, fearful minds and painful bodies, gods and goddesses, and poverty and selves. We use our time on Earth to advise others to listen to, join with, and even temporarily follow whoever and whatever feels happy. Foremost, we encourage all to be their own seers by reconnecting with the power and wisdom of our all-knowing hearts.

We give guidance about the past and offer ways to change our response to it. Our past memories can be changed gradually or all at once from traumatic to tragic to troublesome to trying to triumphant. We then release our life energy to continue its natural flow through ourselves as health, wealth, and happiness. We free ourselves to love our lives and feel our passions now and here. We know our destiny, our future as written in the stars, our Earth walk as Spirit willed from the beginning for all time.

Seers track time back to the very beginning for others and tell them of their past lives. We are able to read from soul records their ancient illnesses and pains as well as their future health and happiness. We are able to see this along with the other person as we look out from this present moment in time. We see what is happening in another's life today because of the past, then track forward into their future and see what they are creating for themselves. We help by showing them different inevitable futures depending on their happiness with their present lifestyles.

Seers become miracle workers when there is the willingness and readiness of another to change their relationship to the past and future and pivot them around a happy today. All of us want to know why we were created in this vast universe and what is going to happen after we die. You ask many questions to avoid answering what it is now that you are here to do on Earth. Life has become making sense of it all. As innocent children we were untroubled in mind by such questions. We trusted our soul to know naturally, effortlessly and instinctively the where and when of our body's movements.

Our soul knows where we are going because it knows where we have been. The self thinks it knows the future based on what it thinks it knows of the past. However, our selves merely externalize, project and make up. Whether as victor or victim, when we live for our selves we cannot see our future. With eyes open or closed, we dream dreadfully of injustices in our past and of punishments in our future. Until one fine day when we realize that our life in the present moment is never actually experienced. When we understand from where we have come and to where we return, we release all fearful thoughts of whom we do not wish, want and will to be.

Seers get to a place in our lives where we become one with all life. We see everything as if it was happening now. When seeing a vision a seer becomes the vision. To us, every action and thought is connected in the past, present and future. We weave the very thread of life as we understand who we are. For us to understand the evolution of the Earth and what is to take place here in the future, we seek to understand our own recurring rebirths into this world.

In ancient times as now, our practical thoughts and our psychic knowing, our alert senses and our natural instincts work perfectly together whenever we rediscover our seemingly lost souls and silent spirits. We realize that our unhappy beliefs are mere veils adorning our hearts' passion for living wisely. Seers work with the energy and power of love within and without us. Whatever we desire with our whole hearts and with our undivided minds, we re-create through our natural bodies.

Many people who come to me for a reading do not actually believe that they deserve what they can manifest or desire. Because seers experience what is unbelievable, we trust what we see, and know rather than believe. Some Spirit workers such as those who channel and scribe can be unbelievers of Spirit and even sceptical of our universe's friendliness. However, seers quickly learn how much more we receive when we relax our mind's resistance and surrender to the truth and beauty of our visions. This is how I see the Spirit world all the time.

For so many others living by their unhappy beliefs, they have to see Spirit first to be happy. Many people believe in God and the Goddess without the awakened vision of seers. If I ask them about Spirit, their explanation is not explicit, it is round and about. Seers today are no different from what other sons of God and daughters of Gaia have always been. Adam and Lilith, Jesus and Mary Magdalene, and Muhammad and Fatima were seers as twinned souls during their inspired Earth walks.

Ancient wisdom is nearly hidden within today's standardized religious works because the original stories of Great Spirit's timeless love and Nature's timely abundance have been overwritten to correspond to victorious and victimised selves in their made-up world of fear and toil. Many in today's work world have watches kept to a common time that we agree will govern our comings and goings. We then wonder why back in ancient times people lived to such a great age. I have visited tribes living naturally away from the madding crowds and met people there who are actively living beyond 100 years. They are not governed by clock time.

Our senses seem to provide evidence for our thoughts of permanent physical death. The seer goes beyond the veil of death and travels into other worlds of our one reality by not energising these false and fearful thoughts. Like the shaman, the seer knows that life is a circle and continuous. When we journey into the worlds of knowing spirits and playful souls, our restless minds and bodies are tended to by our intuition and instincts. Our souls merge into the unlimited reality of the Spirit world while our selves simultaneously retain just the slightest willingness to remain in this world's unreality of limits.

Seers understand that life expresses itself through movement and changes. We move and change with the flow of life in the world of Nature. In the world of selves where problems evade solutions, adults force upon us their schedules and maps which dictate by the time we get to this place we should do that thing. We are then made busy doing things, like schooling, growing up, marrying, parenting, and growing old. What is old? Wisdom is old, and contrary to "the older you get the wiser you become," we were all born with wise hearts yet were likely reared to age as foolish selves.

Since the moment we were conceived in our mothers' wombs, we have been restfully dreaming our heart's eternal knowingness. Cell by cell, our souls imprinted our destiny into our effortlessly forming bodies via life-sustaining instincts inherited from all our ancestors' Earth walks. From some moment before or after we were released from the womb, we began to dream restlessly. We experienced unknowingness, anxiety and trauma in our pristine infant bodies that are created purely to live out our anciently known future.

Always this trauma of the separation of our unborn and undying souls from our suddenly birthed selves is premature. Our selves are birthed by the need to deal with what is unknown to our souls. Mostly this occurs during our unloving nurturing. Our innocent bodies and minds can sense uncaring births and even unhappy pregnancies. We do not know what to do with the violence to our knowingness, since our genetic nature has not prepared us for this. Great Spirit does not will any natural form in the entire universe to experience anxieties of separation, traumatic world passages or unhappy dreams.

What a difference our experience of this world would be if we were naturally allowed to develop the gifts and abilities that we were conceived with in this and all our other lifetimes upon this wondrous Earth. When I see Harry Potter films, I find myself wishing I had been sent to Hogwarts.

I wonder if today's children actually had the choice between Hogwarts or the schools, which they would happily attend. I am aware of only a few private educational systems whose teachers and parents encourage our children's soul connection to Nature and Spirit while developing practical skills for this world's betterment.

Throughout time, all seers and visionaries have worked in this unnatural world by maintaining our connection to the natural and supernatural. For several weeks last year, it was difficult for many sensitive souls to rest because of the explosion of an atomic bomb within the Earth. This unnatural release of energy affected the inner and outer magnetic structure of the Earth, as has every unnatural weapon that men and now women have employed with force beyond their own bodies' natural strength.

As the bomb exploded, I was aware that there would be an earthquake somewhere because of the artificial disturbance of Earth's energies. What happened was a series of earthquakes in Hawaii, which already gets plenty of mild shaking from its volcano. I told David about the upcoming earthquake in Hawaii just as he needed to head back to his heartland for a few months to get a British resident visa processed. Spirit redirected him to visit with Sai Baba in India instead for several weeks until after the earthquake happened. Its epicentre turned out to be 5 miles offshore from where our friends Diane and Guy live and work, both of whom David expected to visit with.

Seers sense what is happening to the Earth. We know what we do to the Earth we do to ourselves. The more we make the Earth sick the sicker we make ourselves. The waste of our planet is happening to our bodies as well. We are the direct result of what is happening to the Earth and that is why there are cancers. We are not here to suffer. We are on a journey of enlightenment, of relearning what it means to use our life force to will and choose freely. Seers live life fully, as if every day was our last day on this beautiful Earth.

Plants and flowers are preparing seeds all the time to continue their expressions of life through renewed forms. This is what natural living is all about. Think of yourself as a seed growing one day into a very big oak tree. This is your spiritual growth. The tree does not stop to think how big it should grow. It keeps on growing. There is nobody telling it to halt, so it reaches its branches into the sky towards the sun as it stretches its roots for the water beneath the earth. When we are as trees, our natural bodies are rooted in the lower world of Nature and our open minds reach for the upper world of Heaven.

Wherever I travel throughout the world, it is from the survivors of ancient cultures that I have learned the simple parables that are glimpses of inner wisdom and knowing. Ancient cultures in different lands from one side of the globe to the other had flourishing systems of healing, spiritual discipline and personal development. Whether they were kahunas or priestesses, seers knowingly helped family, friends and neighbours. These cultures balanced mastery and mystery. Their ways shared the perennial seership wisdom and were taught orally. They honoured men and women equally.

Throughout written history and especially in recent centuries, seership wisdom has been distorted from the original knowing of who we are and from where we have come. I have had the blessing to learn directly from the Australian and New Zealand aboriginals before they disappear, as have their nearby Tasmanian cousins and many of their distant American relations. The same has been and will be the fate of our native plants, animals and peoples whenever Earthly forms of divine innocence seem to threaten this world's guilt-ridden progress.

As I write, the families who live in an ancient Egyptian village on the west bank of the Nile are all being moved from their temples and houses that are built upon and amongst their millenniums old ancestor's graves. Nearby, a massive new village for them and other displaced guardians is under construction in the name of 21st century progress. I have seen a vision of hotels built on their former ancestral home sites because this real estate is none other than the guardian lands to the Valley of Kings. Now is not too late to know as seers what is happening in this world.

I wonder what would have happened if we had continued to follow an Earth-centred path of the Goddess and the Heaven-inspired wisdom of God, as I remember from the time before Christianity. We lived a life of love, laughter and joy while practicing our pagan traditions. We celebrated our sense of connectedness with heartfelt communal ceremonies. What would have happened if that had continued in this world today? What would our experience have been without all the holocausts?

Because so many of us have experienced those painful past lives, we have returned now to be healed and to demonstrate that every one of us has the power within to live happily on this Earth. We are all able to travel backwards and forwards in time. You already time travel most evenings when asleep. During our sleep we naturally journey into the worlds of our one reality. Sleep is for renewing our connection with all of creation and with the one Creator. As you would expect, however, our troubled minds and ailing bodies chain us to a nightmarish middle world whether our eyes are open or shut.

During trouble-free sleep we receive healing knowledge that surpasses the understanding of our practical minds. Life becomes a happy dream when we knowingly anticipate what has not yet expressed through us into this world. Our happiness can be permanent, and every single one of us can share in the good life. We glimpse eternal bliss as we merge with Spirit through our heart to understand as seers that there is life after death, that this Earth is an amazing and beautiful place and that the creation of divinely happy human beings is the purpose of the universe.

Are we preparing for the life or lives ahead of us? Have we resolved our past or pasts? Are we ready to pass from this chaotic working world into a place of perfect peace and play? Are we ready to experience our immortality for a bit longer as divine humans living naturally in this awakened world? Some of us already prepare for the passing of our bodies while living on Earth as if we were going to live forever in this world. We do live forever, but not in any world where we are minded to believe in scarcity.

We come into this world grasping nothing and we go out of this world empty-handed. Children of all ages remind us that we never need to hold onto any thing or thought longer than is practical, comfortable and natural during our Earth passage. It is most unnatural to strive in this world to accumulate and possess for our selves what is shared freely amongst our souls. At the end of our experience of time, what we have ever held onto will be seen to be the very thought or thing that postponed our reawakening to our openhearted and open-handed souls. God and the Goddess are welcomed back into the sanctuary of our inner power, into our spacious and gentle hearts where our souls never left.

Through seership we understand ourselves, our husbands and wives, our children, those we live and work with, and our neighbours near and far. Scientists claim we use 10% of our brain for our sensing body when controlled by our thinking mind. That is good news because the other 90% is available for the energy of Spirit to express through our natural bodies. If we were to balance the usage of our logical left brain, which we spend much of our time thinking from every day, with that of our creative right brain, where imagination and intuition is available at all times, we would bring into this world our psychic gifts every day.

Our inner mind of infinite knowing and eternal wisdom and our outer mind of the practical thoughts of our self-centred world could be in harmony for the moment. Our amazing intuition comes from the energy of our heart centre and is processed through the matter of our mind, the brain. When our hearts guide us we are in a balanced, loving, relaxed yet alert state of being, ready to accept Spirit's visions. We feel the divine breath of Creator breathing through us, willing us to live with each inspiration.

Many people owe their lives to visions, dreams and premonitions. Miracles happen every moment, whether you believe or not. They are our momentary experiences of our eternal reality. Love comes to us, but we cannot receive it with effort. We surrender to love, live for love and fall in love. We love our attractive and healthy bodies. We love our open and peaceful minds.

For years I wanted and sought love from others. I understand now that love comes to us from within. I now know that I give to my beloveds the love I receive from the Beloved of my heart. I receive from my beloveds the soul love I give. We are loved as we love. It does not matter whether we love ourselves first or last, as long as in all relationships we feel loved by our souls while we love other souls and selves. We change our relationship with ourselves, and in so doing we love all others with no expectations. We open up to receive love and to accept healing of emotions which have been closed off for so long. We stop fighting ourselves. We are no longer our own worst enemies when we stop looking to others for what seems lacking within ourselves.

We then understand the love of God and the Goddess, our divine masculine and feminine natures. Soul mates come to play and rest together with us. Our soul feels our self's pains and our way out of pain. Souls have only happiness as the answer to whatever form unhappiness appears as. Souls meeting selves, whether oneself or other selves, bring love in the forms it will be received. These forms are birthed in our hearts, the space where selves feel lost and our souls feel at Home. When a soul meets a self, its own or a seeming other, it has no choice whether to reject it or fall in love. Our souls are always in love, always resting and playing at Spirit's will.

When a seer meets another seer, when wholeness meets holiness, we need do nothing but share our happiness. We share a smile, a kiss, a memory, a laugh, a drink, a meal, a smoke, an evening or a lifetime. Souls mirror happiness when together. Souls see healed bodies, peaceful minds, and happy hearts. Seers gaze upon the working world with inner eyes while glimpsing it as selves see. Souls simultaneously see healed hearts and traumatized minds and bodies. Souls see trauma as healed because souls know only how to love. Seers sense outwardly our own and other selves suffering, while simultaneously seeing inwardly our wholeness.

Spirit has written this book through me for those of us who have gone through experiences sometimes so heartbreaking that we wonder how we managed to keep going. In our deepest moments came the inspiration that brings us out of the darkness where we learn the most about who we are not and into the light of our inner knowing, our intuition and our psychic gifts. We gain a deeper understanding of who we are. Everything that has happened and will happen is for a purpose. We are fulfilling our destiny.

I have no worldly qualifications except my many life experiences in this world. I seldom meet medicine men and wise women who have qualifications after their names. If you are looking for someone to help you love life, work with someone who does not say you must do this and must do that. What I write about in this book and the other books that Spirit has already given me to write, will not tell you what you must do. I will only encourage you to find out what your purpose is in life. The people who have helped me the most are not the ones who have shouted the loudest, say they know everything or use fancy words.

Many people have said to me that they were confused by what a particular person is saying or that the book they were reading is so complicated. Keep It Simple Sweetheart. This is a very practical teaching from the worlds of Spirit and Nature. When we do not complicate things and learn to trust, we are prepared to meet another of our soul's mates, another angel. I have a picture of Jesus with his heart aflame. His is a sincere human heart that will never fail. Seers work from the same heart centre of unconditional love. You will sense, feel and know without doubt the happiness and validity of a seer. Seers do not need to say many words, although we sometimes do, because we listen to Spirit voices that speak volumes of wisdom.

We are our own greatest teachers, but selves do not see this when they externalise and project. As our own seers we learn to trust the power that lives within us when we recognize it outside us in Nature and from happy souls of all ages. When we stop denying the messages given to us through our intuition and instincts we see plainly life's simplicity. We understand that life goes way beyond the grave. We distinguish real power from its unnatural illusions. We see and sense how to live happily.

Know when you look into the mirror you are seeing your greatest teacher. The sure way to find your genuine teacher in the world is to develop true qualities within yourself. The power to understand, recognise and know is always with us. Seership is the natural outcome of continuing the abandoned or aborted development of our psychic abilities. We simply remind ourselves of the easy and natural way we lived with the Spirit world during infancy. We remember our own souls and soul mates from the worlds we played and rested with. We feel happy while we hold onto our vision of remembered oneness. In our happiness we are free to love our selves unconditionally.

Selves can defend, upset and harm themselves and others. Selves cannot love themselves or others. Our hearts do. Our healed selves clearly see with our inner eyes that no body or thing will knowingly hurt us. We know when we experience trauma of mind or body that its cause must be from ones who know not their souls. Whether it is our selves or others who have forgotten who we are, the seer's response reflects the Spirit world's miracle of forgiveness. We become our own healers. We are ready to step out into the world to help others because we have helped ourselves.

All the ancient mystery schools taught the first and final lesson of our Earth walk: Know thy Spirit to know thy soul to know thy self. That wisdom is in our hearts. It is our inner being and teacher. When we truly love ourselves it is because we have remembered our oneness with all. We know again, as if for the last time, our completion in the One. The student was ready, the seer did appear and healing happened naturally, miraculously and happily. We were ready as a student of our inner life. The teacher of the heart path comes to us from without until we know again our inner seer. We then stop being students of our selves and again become teachers of our own hearts.

We no longer teach the selfish lessons that we needed to learn alone, yet tried to give to others as greed, envy, hatred, the lot of what we did not want to keep for our selves. We are freed up to gift our soul lessons to others who are willing and ready for happiness. Often, we look to seers, gurus and other masters of heart ways to teach us. We can be of help and are here to help, but spiritualisation comes by one's own willingness and readiness. It does not matter how many people, places and practices we seek out to remind us of who we are. Gurus and ashrams, shamans and sun dances, mystical rituals and magical tools, abstinences and indulgences, wisdom books and tantric workshops may be of great help when we sense we are ready but are not sure for what.

Yet we finally attain inner peace by our own willingness to reconnect our minds and bodies to our hearts. When we bring forth our inner gifts and know the oneness with all things we become enlightened beyond recognition to our selves. We are born again in our natural bodies returned to their health and our opened minds returned to their innocence. This is the gift of the heart, the living flame. Then our work begins to encourage others that divine happiness is not just for the few, but for all.

It is a bit like being a connecting link to another website. During a reading, if I inform another of her ten past lives, it is because I am seeing all these links to all these websites and am able to access them all at once. I see where past life issues are and where healing was and still is being called for. I connect from my self to my soul and spirits to your spirits and soul to your self. This is how beloveds communicate naturally. I have looked into many religions, spiritual practices, and beliefs. All paths of Heart lead us Home, some narrowly, others quite scenically.

My life is a walkabout with beloved spirits and souls on this lovely Earth. If I were to narrow it down, mine is a Nature tradition of walking the land, living in harmony with the Earth and Her people and honouring every natural thing Spirit blesses with sacred breath. All life is a part of me and I live with the tiniest creature, which has every right to be on Earth as I have. When we develop our gift of seership and travel our timelines we know that there is no immediate prospect of this beautiful Earth coming to a man-made end. In all the many visions I have seen throughout my lifetime I always had a sense, feeling and knowing that the Earth will continue.

I have not seen the doom and gloom that others predict. I feel that their own negativity is limiting their inner sensing. I have flown from Europe to the USA hundreds of times and I do see recently out of the plane windows the ice packs drifting much further south than they did decades ago. I have also scuba dived over the last decade at many of the most beautiful sites within the oceans and seas on this planet and have witnessed the decline of colourful fishes and decimation of coral reefs. So what can we do when we hear talk of global warming and such things?

We go out in Nature and within to Spirit. We listen once again. We learn from our first teachers, the elements of the land, waters, wind and sun. Our Earth naturally evolves and seemingly reacts ever more abruptly to this unnatural world's order. I have seen both Nature's sensible abundance and human's senseless poverty throughout our planet. We can change what we say and do right now. We can use energy efficient solutions for heating our homes and for transporting our goods, services and selves. We are evolving our lifestyles to synchronize with the whole world as we will know it after 2012.

I am sitting here at this moment in time, late winter, doing the final touches to this book from the heart of Britain. As I look out on Nature, it is raining and the wind is gusting. It is a clearing time, a time for us to see clearly who we are, to cleanse our selves and to sweep out the inner home of our true being. It really is our time to wake up and discover who we are and who we are not. We are not the conditioning, control and manipulation that have happened to us in this lifetime. We are beautiful, whole and incredible children of this universe of life.

As walkers between all the worlds, seers bring spiritual and natural alertness, our intuitions and instincts, into our everyday lives. We are aware of what we eat and where we dispose of our rubbish. That is all part of being a seer. To live spiritedly in the 21st century, we become responsible for the cause and effect of our actions. What we do to the Earth we do to ourselves. If the Earth is hurting then so are we, and when we are not happy all of creation misses our soulfulness.

We see what is happening to the Earth and what is happening to ourselves. We understand that we are all related. As I drive the motorway in good weather I wonder who else is noticing the trees, the animals in the fields, the birds and the sky. Are they too busy talking on their mobile phones, listening to their satellite navigation system or even watching television while driving? People are not sensitive to what is going on around them because they are not using their intuition and instincts, their inner knowing and sensing.

The Spirit world does not seem to come through to them as when they were children. They do not give spirits a chance to. The only time Spirit is allowed to connect with them is when they are asleep. When they wake up at three in the morning, lying and wondering what is happening, it is because this is the only time their ancestors and descendants in the Spirit world can be heard, seen and felt by them. Their lives are just so full and so busy. Yet just in time for our 2012 opportunity to rid this world again of its unhappiness, an amazing conscious awareness is growing.

At the festivals and shows I attend, more and more people are looking for other people who can help them and who they can help. Going Home again, smile by loving smile, touch by healing touch, and two by two. Life really is this simple. By means of our imagination, inspiration and intuition from the Spirit world, we gradually ascend into seeing the information that has to do with our human and cosmic evolution. When we have fully developed our psychic gifts we can see and explain the evolution of our souls and other souls between the veil of an old death and a new birth. Seers awaken to our completed soul memory and learn from our experiences instead of requiring more practice, repetition and ritual.

Imagine this entire universe to be like an orchestra with you as the conductor. When our minds and bodies are absolutely in unison with our hearts we play the most amazing music for all the worlds to hear. We are no longer just practicing. We are conducting energy, the creation of one life as many sounds. Spirit wills that we are all able to tap into this consciousness. When we return to our childhood innocence, we become transparent like a band of light to natural wisdom and supernatural knowledge. You do not have our pure beginner's mind when you are burdened by worldly problems. To see clearly, have no trouble in mind, step out of the way, and welcome the heart worlds back in.

You seek so diligently until you again find rest in the upper world of Spirit. Through the Beloved's visions, we see our seemingly lost Spirit guides, gods and goddesses. We gratefully realize that we have always had within us all the help we ever needed to bring happiness through our selves into this world. We may merely have forgotten our childhood experiences of playing with supposedly mythical unicorns and dragons in the lower world of our souls. When our inner eyes have closed we no longer know what we no longer see.

Our middle world of limits is soulless and dispirited without these wonderful Spirit beings and very real soul family of the fairies, elementals and other friends I played with as a little girl. I remember life in its natural ease and know it is not reflected in today's laborious world. If I can help make it so, seers, wizards and witches from my land and all lands will not become mythical creatures in the world of our future. Your destiny can be as mine, to see a happy Earth through the open eyes of your inner seer.

Exercise 10   SEEING OUR EARTH

Of all the profound stories I could still share of my magical time in Egypt while writing this book, I will leave you with a simple gift from our heart brother, Khalid.

Khalid's grandfather was the village sheik, the seer, throughout Khalid's life until he passed over a few years ago. The moment I first met Khalid and before we were introduced, I felt his grandfather's amazing presence next to me. I asked the friendly men visiting with Khalid whom this holy man I was sensing was coming forth to speak with. The Spirit world drew me to Khalid as the one to meet, so I described the spirit I was seeing to him.

Slowly and knowingly Khalid smiled, introduced himself and thanked me for being the first one to confirm the presence of his grandfather that he had been recently sensing with greater urgency. It was a beautiful reunion of spirits in Heaven and Earth. The sheik affirmed Khalid's readiness to assume his hereditary seership responsibilities. This was the first of our many visits during the next three months from the Heart royalty of these ancient lands of mystery and mastery.

Khalid shared with us the significance of growing up with his extended family in the mud-bricked homes that are being demolished daily, as quickly as his relatives relocate to the new village nearby. I never learned the actual age of these homes. When he invited us there to meet his lovely Egyptian family, the well-built and time-honoured community houses seemed to be as ancient as the 800-year-old homesteads in Old Oriibi on Third Mesa of the Hopi lands.

Khalid often visited with us in our magnificent flat in the grand house that he built for his English wife Rainya during their former marriage. Many of the fond memories Khalid shared with us were of the trusting ways of his community during his childhood. As he was taking his unhurried leave through our terrace doorway one afternoon, he glanced down at the shiny brass latch on his elegantly shaped wood door and widened his already beaming smile. He described how the ancient Egyptians ingeniously designed large wooden latches for their heavy wood doors. Khalid told us this type of wood latch was still on the original door of his father's house where he was born and raised.

I pictured what he described as similar to the huge wooden planks barring castle doors of Europe. Khalid insisted we understood one detail. Midway along the wood latch is a notch to fit snugly a carved wooden peg, the house key. When the door was open, the peg in the notch kept the latch in place and out of the way.

Khalid's beautiful smile broke into a moment's private laughter. From the time he was born to that very morning when he had looked in on his parents, he had never seen the peg move. The door of his ancestor's home remained unlocked during the 30 years of his life. It will likely remain unlatched in a few months' time when the cherished house gives up its ghosts.

Khalid's fate is moving his wife, children and parents into the new complex with running water, electricity, heating and cooling, and other modern conveniences. His destiny as a seer is unfolding as well. When seen together, Khalid's destiny modifies his fate, transforming the apparent negativity of leaving behind a simpler and trusting lifestyle into an opportunity to bring ancient ways of seership into the 21st century.

For our final exercise, it is up to you where you go and what techniques you use to connect with Spirit and your soul to answer the following related questions. What does the future hold for you? What vision does your inner seer reveal for bringing your rediscovered seership gifts and abilities into this world? How do you see your destiny on Earth based on your present life? Are you willing and ready to be an integral part of the solution to our world's problems by the year 2012?

We change the fate of the Earth through the knowing visions of our all-seeing Heart. We dream as happy souls and hear our wise spirits. We feel our eternal unity with Heaven and Nature. With courage and gratitude we gaze as seers upon our lovely Earth and come Home together, as we were in the beginning.

EARTH GAZING SEERS

I have heard the whispers of the moon
As I danced around the sun,
Speaking words of wisdom
In an old and ancient tongue.

Father Sky awaits us
In every star that's born,
To see the beauty of our souls
And know that we are one.

Let me show you where the seas meet,
Only you will know how deep.
The flow of fate into destiny
Is our love's greatest feat.

Within our heartfelt passion
Comes a song that is so sweet
Of joy, of love, of laughter.
It is you, who needs to meet

Your soul as if for the last time
Without your pain and grief.
It's time to shed all past lives
And wake up from your deep sleep.

I see which way your path lies,
Only you may know how far
Is the journey within which takes you
To life's purpose and desire.

Mother Earth is calling you
To come within Her womb.
For dancing to Her heartbeat
Will release you from your tomb.

Deep within your heart space
Is a place of sacred fire,
Of mystery and magic,
Which the elements inspire.

We are the seers
Gazing on the Earth.
The Heart of All Knowing
Is our place of rebirth

To a new way of living,
From self to soul to heart.
Open up the doorways,
Come, let's start

Sky dancing as beloveds
With grace and ease, enthralled.
The love of our selves
Is the mastery of all.

Written by Barbara Meiklejohn-Free,
inspired by Charles Anthony

BARBARA'S AFTER WORD

BY CASSANDRA EASON

Seership is a universal gift, found in different ages and cultures with remarkably similar practices and that uses remarkably similar tools. For the tools of Seership are essentially the gifts of Mother Nature, given to us freely if we can become aware of them. If we can open this side of ourselves we no longer wander unguided, seemingly following random impulses and events and unaware of our own power to control our lives and destiny. For from the first explorations of seership we can begin to establish once more the forgotten connection with the Spiritual guardians who have been with us since childhood when we needed no teaching to walk between and within the different worlds.

But as adults, the everyday world intrudes and our souls can become buried beneath the noise and relentless pace of modern life. This soul loss is well understood by the shamans of indigenous cultures from Siberia to sub Saharan Africa. However in today's 24/7 frantic dash from one activity to another, in search of what we imagine is fulfilment of our spiritual hunger, soul loss may be manifest as a constant craving for even more action or stimulation to fill the void. We can also so easily lose meaningful communication with our soul families who travel with us through the generations and so we can feel alienated and alone and unable to accept the love of those who have loved us in different roles in different lifetimes.

Modern medicine seeks to fix the body without any reference to the soul that may be calling out for validation and manifesting its distress in physical symptoms. These symptoms may become worse with side effects of potentially toxic so called pharmaceutical wonders that can unbalance and weaken our natural restorative and self healing powers.

Seership is the gift we all possess, forgotten from childhood magical insights, but still there that we can put together all the pieces of the jigsaw of our lives scattered in so many directions. Having walked though the pages of this book and stopped to pick up keys to unlocking your own innate potential, you may realise that the knowledge was there all the time deep within you, familiar but forgotten or distrusted and disbelieved. For if we can empower ourselves to put the jigsaw together piece by piece, using the tools of Seership, exploring the exercises that reawaken the connections and the recollections, then we can slowly begin to heal ourselves. We can see relationships in the context of many lifetimes, understand why we feel that some people are soul family or even mates and trust this connection to guide us to them in this life or accept for whatever reason it cannot be this time round. We can recall and avoid the mistakes and heal past traumas that seemed irrational, but in fact are old hurts that need acknowledging and sometimes put behind us in this lifetime, because they are holding us back from moving towards trust and hope.

The guardians and guides are patiently waiting as they have always been and once we are able to reopen the pathways to those other dimensions, then we can hear their wisdom. What is more through their guidance we can use those now accessible parts of the mind and soul to heal ourselves, through knowing the love and support of our wise ancestors? As with Barbara you may find one place above all others is the doorway to this connection. For Barbara the mysterious pyramids were a significant gateway, but for others it may be a forest, an old stone circle, a medicine wheel, a labyrinth or a pool of water in a mundane setting made wondrous by moonlight.

Some of you may go on to work in healing, as spiritual practitioners or chanellers of ancient wisdom. For others the path that opens when you close these pages may be one of personal healing and making sense of a family or personal loss and seeing that life goes on and souls return to renew the kinship. You may discover your guides and angels and through them give others wise advice, healing and comfort.

For Seership is the oldest and deepest of arts but one that once you are given those keys seems totally natural, totally part of the modern world, a world no longer in black and white but brilliant colours. No longer is there the sense of separation from animal wisdom, nature spirits or Mother Nature herself the wisest of teachers. She speaks if we listen through the wind in the trees, the water rushing over stones and the clouds that form images high in the sky.

We do need books and teachers to remind us of and help us reclaim our ancient heritage and so you may choose to go back to this book several times, trying the exercises to new depths of enlightenment as you become naturally more in tune with your own spiritual nature over the weeks and months ahead.

We can reclaim our own souls and teach the next generation not to hand theirs over so readily to live instead through simulated technological wonders and experience the world by proxy through televisions, DVDS and computer consoles. For though we think of seers as ancient wise men and women or through the modern television hyped mediumship, the reality is that it is a sacred gift within the grasp of us all. Once we can see clearly with our spiritual eyes, anything becomes possible, nothing impossible. We can see beyond the immediate, the illusory and the temporary, to experience a deep connection with those spiritual beings we can see and hear sharing our space, but in another more ethereal dimension that our living spirits can enter now and for always.

As you read the experiences in this book you realise that life is not a jigsaw after all, but an interconnected web of experience and that every experience has meaning, every meeting when we follow our instincts and psychic promptings is for a purpose. What is more we can use those people earthly and spiritual to whom we are drawn quite naturally to help us not just to see but to make the destiny that is right for us and so to make our mark with our footprints in life's sands

Once we can see the road which was there all along we can walk it in our unique way and our own pace. Some will travel rapidly spiritually to the stars, others be content to sit and watch the myriad butterfly patterns of life unfold and to weave a tapestry of experience based in the here and now, but always aware of and touched by the blessings of the spiritual world all around. We are spiritual creatures in a spiritual body and all have the potential to become wise men and women, the true purpose of Seership

Cassandra Eason, March 2007

ACKNOWLEDGMENTS

Firstly, to my twin flame, my beloved husband David, who has helped me to write this book by spending endless hours on the computer putting together and making sense of my dyslexic words, grammar, and spelling. Thank you from my heart and soul, you saw the vision and became the voice of love.

To Jacqui, my dear friend and editor, for spending days and nights working on all the voice tapes and transferring them onto the computer. I can never thank you enough.

To Dennis my spiritual dad, who is a master magician and healer, thank you for your love and support.

To John my publisher, thank you for believing in me and for seeking me out to write my book. I would never have done it without you.

To Adam and Suzanne, my managers and agents, thank you for helping me with my book with your words of support and encouragement BB.

To my brother Jim and Catherine, thank you for finding me and being the greatest gift of all, my family, and for my special Niece Sonia and her family all my love.

To Olivia, Mark and my spirit daughter Tula, in Hawaii, words cannot express how much I love you all.

To Brenda, you are the greatest, and to my dear friend Ocean thank you for making me laugh. To Pat, my close friend, thanks for listening and being a shoulder to cry on.

To my ex-husband Shaun and his wife Sally, lots of love.

To my ex-partner James, thank you for helping me on to my next step of evolution, from self to soul, until we meet again, eternal love and thanks.

To Lynn C, Barbara, Sky, Scotty, Rondie,Yuri, my sister and brother soul mates, you are forever in my heart. Love never dies. Until we meet again.

To Alan and Jenny, Annie and Terry, Debs and Lui, John and Elaine, Gavin, Joyaa and Scarlet, Karen and Michael, Tim and Nat, Carrie and Ian, big hugs and kisses to my extended family.

To Jennifer, Fiona, Clair, Victoria ,Glynis, Jan, Bobana, Cat, Fiona, Emma, Joanne, Cara, Marjory, Maya, Millie, Sara, Sally, Tamerin, Kate, all wonderful girlfriends xx

To everyone at the College of Psychic Studies, a big thank you, especially Max and Octavia.

A very big thank you to everyone at all the shows I do, especially Peter and Lee, Nina and Barry, Mike and Hazel, for all your help, support and healing. From exhibitors to organisers, you are in my thoughts always, sees you soon.

To Teri my dear friend and fellow witch from Salem, What would you like me to do with all the wood? love you BB.

To all my USA Family, Silvia, Dancing Hands, Cynthy,Betty Jane, dear sisters thank you.

Love and blessings to Ralph and Audrey Harvey thank you for sharing so much BB

To my spirit family in Australia, Joyce and Gordon and Lee and Mark, Miss you xx

To Pauline and Sid in Spain, blessings of love and joy, thank you.

Special thanks to the following nine authors and friends
who endorsed my book.

Philip Gardiner www.gardinersworld.com
Ross Heaven www.thefourgates.com
Becky Walsh www.lightofspirit.co.uk
Cassandra Eason www.cassandraeason.co.uk
Edwin Courtenay www.edwincourtenay.co.uk
Donald McKinney www.celticcircle.com
Sandra Ingerman www.shamanicvisions.com
Yuri Geller www.uri-geller.com
Jackie Newcomb www.jackynewcomb.co.uk

BOOKS

O books
O is a symbol of the world, of oneness and unity. In different cultures it also means the "eye", symbolizing knowledge and insight, and in Old English it means "place of love or home". O books explores the many paths of understanding which different traditions have developed down the ages, particularly those today that express respect for the planet and all of life.

For more information on the full list of over 300 titles please visit our website **www.O-books.net**

myspiritradio is an exciting web, internet, podcast and mobile phone global broadcast network for all those interested in teaching and learning in the fields of body, mind, spirit and self development. Listeners can hear the show online via computer or mobile phone, and even download their favourite shows to listen to on MP3 players whilst driving, working, or relaxing.

Feed your mind, change your life with O Books, The O Books radio programme carries interviews with most authors, sharing their wisdom on life, the universe and everything...e mail questions and co-create the show with O Books and myspiritradio.

Just visit **www.myspiritradio.com** for more information.